CHOOSE IT to LOSE IT!

CHOOSE IT to LOSE IT!

The Ultimate Pocket Guide to Save 500 Calories a Day!

With Amy Brightfield

Oxmoor House.

CONTENTS

Choose it!
**BERRIES &
BROWNED
BUTTER WAFFLES**
239
CALORIES

Choose it!
BEEF TACOS
320
CALORIES

Choose it!
LIGHT CHOCOLATE
CHIP COOKIES
96
CALORIES

When it comes to successfully losing weight and consistently eating well, the secret is **MAKING THE RIGHT CHOICES.**

And when we say choices, we aren't talking about picking a bland turkey sandwich over the cheeseburger you're craving. We mean opting for a hearty burger with toppings that has 300 fewer calories. Or going to your favorite Italian restaurant and ordering pasta, but customizing the rest of your meal—and even the dish—so you eat 400 calories less than you typically would. You can absolutely ditch extra calories and eat better without sacrificing what your taste buds crave.

Choose It to Lose It is a real-world guide to effort-lessly downsizing your calorie count. Cutting calories, followed by regular exercise, is the most effec-tive way to kick-start weight loss, and making better-for-you food decisions through-out the day can easily save you 100 calories at breakfast or 70 on a drink—leading you to cut 300 to 500 calories a day without even thinking about it. You'll discover that small changes like these, made every day, can add up to losing 10 or 20 pounds a year, and keep you eating better for a lifetime.

This book helps you make smart choices no matter where you find yourself—whether you're in the snack aisle, at the drive-thru, or in front of your own fridge. The best part: **THIS BOOK WORKS WITH ANY DIET...**

Each chapter in this book offers suggestions on easy ways to avoid calorie bombs. There are tips on making any meal more nutritious, delicious recipe makeovers from *Cooking Light* magazine, and hundreds of healthier options to consider when you are on the go or at your favorite chain restaurant. Dip in and out of the book and use the information that makes sense for your lifestyle. There is no one-size-fits-all formula for everyone. If you want to start small, try making simple changes for one meal, and then eventually for all of them. Research tells us that long-term behavior change is the result of small victories and little daily tweaks over a long period of time. Incorporate healthier eating choices, one at a time, until they become rou-tine, and you'll be headed to a trimmer waistline in no time.

did you know?

DOWNSIZING YOUR DISHES CAN HELP YOU EAT LESS | Participants in a Cornell University study were given 34- or 17-ounce bowls for their ice cream. Those with the bigger bowls dished out 31% more.

7 NUTRITION MYTHS BUSTED

With all the conflicting nutrition advice out there, it's easy to get flustered when you're trying to make good food choices. We clear the air on seven nutrition myths that could be hampering your decisions—not to mention standing between you and your favorite foods!

1. Fried foods are always fatty.

the truth is: It depends how you fry it. More nutritious coatings like panko crumbs and wholewheat flour help, as does the temperature at which you fry. For most foods, 375° is optimal; oil temperatures that are too low will cause foods to soak up more oil, increasing the amount of calories and fat.

2. Organic foods are more nutritious.

the truth is: Organic foods aren't inherently more nutritious, although there are many good reasons to choose organic. Research has shown that there's no significant nutritional difference between conventional and organic crops and livestock. There is, of course, still the issue of trace amounts of pesticides and herbicides, so wash conventional produce carefully.

3. Eating eggs raises your cholesterol.

the truth is: Dietary cholesterol, or cholesterol found in foods including eggs, doesn't greatly affect your body's cholesterol levels. What does? Saturated and trans fat, and one large egg has no trans fat and only 1.5g saturated fat.

4. A product with a health claim is always better for you.

the truth is: Sometimes the claims don't tell the whole story. A bag of chips that's "made with whole grains" is still a bag of chips. Many specific health claims, such as "lowers cholesterol," are usually carefully regulated but others aren't. What you really have to check is the ingredients list and Nutrition Facts Panel to see if the health claims add up.

5. If you're trying to lose weight, you should stop snacking.

the truth is: Snacking helps tame hunger by keeping your blood sugar and metabolism on an even keel. So you should definitely make room for one or two nutritious and satisfying snacks per day. Turn to the Snacks and Sweets chapter (page 152) for more ideas.

6. Adding salt to the pot adds a lot of sodium to the food.

the truth is: The percentage of sodium absorbed is small, and salt added to boiling water can make vegetables more nutritious by stopping nutrients from leaching into the water.

7. The most nutritious vegetables are brightly-colored.

the truth is: Disease-fighting nutrients give vegetables their vivid colors but white counts, too! Cauliflower, onion, and garlic all contain compounds linked to a lower risk of cancer.

HOW TO CHOOSE IT TO LOSE IT

The key to making long-lasting changes to your diet is to be well-informed about all your food choices, whether you're shopping at the grocery store or grabbing a bite at your favorite restaurant. To lose weight, you have to burn more calories than you take in. And while it's important to exercise regularly and weave as much activity as possible into your daily life (take the stairs instead of the elevator, park as far away as possible when you're running errands), the other big half of the equation is eating the right amount of calories and fat. That doesn't mean butter, cream, salt, or sugar should be MIA in your meals. The big picture of healthy eating means everything in moderation. For adults, experts have recommended daily caps on salt (aim for less than 2,300mg a day, under 1,500 mg if you're 51 or older or have high blood pressure, diabetes or chronic kidney disease), sugar (less than 25 grams of *added* sugar), and fat: no more than 20% to 35% of your calories should come from fat, with the majority of those fats being the good kind, including poly- and monounsaturated, and limiting saturated fat. Of course, these are general guidelines, and you should have a conversation with your doctor or a dietitian to determine exactly what your personal limits should be.

Knowing your own parameters will help you make smart food choices, track what you consume, and have what you want while still eating healthy. Cooking at home is the easiest way to make sure you keep within your limits, but it's not realistic

did you know?

DON'T CUT TOO MUCH | Having too few calories—below 1,200 per day—can backfire and cause your metabolism to slow down to preserve the calories you are eating.

to think that you'll never eat out. In the pages that focus on dining out, our goal is to help you eat smart, given your options at that particular restaurant. Just keep in mind how your choices at the drive-thru or a restaurant figure into your calorie, fat, salt, and sugar intake for the day.

Sound like a tall order? Know that making better-for-you food decisions is easier than ever, thanks to the TONS of options out there, not only when you're food shopping to cook at home, but also when you eat out. Most restaurants and fast food places have healthier picks highlighted and grouped together on the menu in some way. Keep in mind that *fried, creamy,* and *crispy* are generally flags that mean the dish isn't the healthiest. In most cases, you can also customize your order to minimize the calories and fat—all you have to do is ask. Don't hesitate to request grilled instead of fried, sauce on the side, or going light on the oil, butter, or cheese. And sharing is always a good idea, especially when it comes to dessert! Almost all fast food places have their nutrition information posted online or in a pamphlet at the restaurant, but it's best to read up beforehand so you're armed with information, or even your meal plan, when it's time to place your order.

Using this book as a guide, you can easily save calories at every meal and snack. And everything adds up: Since 3,500 calories equals about one pound, burning 3,500 more calories than you take in can, on average, lead to losing one pound. So, aiming to axe about 500 calories from your diet each day can help you shed about one pound per week. That may sound like a snail's pace, but research shows that going gradually, and losing one to two pounds per week is the best path to slimming down—and changing your eating habits—for good.

6 STEPS TO HEALTHY EATING SUCCESS

As you use the swaps in this book to guide your food choices, keep these six pointers in mind:

1. Start small.

Habits don't change overnight, so it's best to tackle one not-so-healthy eating habit at a time and go slow. So, for example, if you're aiming to cut back on soda and currently have two a day, first limit yourself to one each day, then one every other day, and so on.

2. Read food labels.

The two most important features to pay attention to: Nutrition Facts and the ingredients list. These both clue you in to what you're really eating. In fact, studies show that people who read the Nutrition Facts Panel are more likely to eat fewer foods that are high in saturated fat—a type of fat that contributes not only to weight gain but also to heart disease and diabetes. The Nutrition Facts Panel lists the calories, calories from fat, total fat, saturated fat, trans fat, protein, carbohydrates, fiber, sugar, cholesterol, sodium, vitamins A and C, calcium, and iron per serving. Many companies also include additional information, such as levels of potassium and mono- and polyunsaturated fats. To use the Nutrition Facts Panel correctly, pay close attention to the serving information. Often, a package or bottle will contain several servings, which means that you have to limit yourself to the serving size and/or multiply the calorie, fat, sodium, and sugar grams by the number of servings you're eating. The ingredient list tells you what was used to make that food.

Nutrition Facts	
Serving Size 1/2 cup (28g)	
Servings Per Container About 4.5	
Amount Per Serving	
Calories 120	Calories from Fat 15
	% Daily Value*
Total Fat 2g	3%
Saturated Fat 0g	0%
Trans Fat 0g	
Cholesterol 0mg	0%
Sodium 70mg	3%
Total Carbohydrate 23g	8%
Dietary Fiber 1g	6%
Sugars 15g	
Protein 2g	

In general, the shorter the list, the less processed the food is—and that's a good thing. Also remember that ingredients are listed by volume, so whichever ingredient comes first is what the food contains the most of.

3. No forbidden foods.

You know the saying "absence makes the heart grow fonder"? Well, it applies to food, too. Banning, say, chocolate ice cream, is a surefire way to find yourself in front of the freezer late one night, spoon in hand, poised to eat whatever pint of ice cream crosses your path. You absolutely have to make room for your favorite foods in your everyday eating or else you'll just end up going overboard once you do give in to a craving. Keep "trigger foods"—or foods that you can't stop eating once you start—out of the house and designate a time (maybe once a week) that you'll indulge.

4. Don't skip meals.

It might seem like a good idea to save calories, but missing a meal means you're going hours without eating, and you'll just be hungrier and more likely to binge when you do finally eat. If you know you'll be having a big dinner, eat small meals or snacks throughout the day to keep your energy high and your appetite in check.

5. Watch portion size.

Just as important as knowing what's in your food is keeping tabs on how much you're eating. Being familiar with what reasonable servings of protein, carbohydrates, and fats look like is crucial, especially since restaurants often have out-of-control portions. Use visual cues, such as 3 ounces of cooked meat = a deck of cards or 1 cup of soup = a baseball to help you accurately eyeball a serving.

6. Cook more.

Even if you can only squeeze in time to grab a pan a few times a week, cooking at home will help you lose weight. People typically consume 50% more calories when eating out, and restaurant dishes can often pack an entire day's worth of saturated fat and calories.

SAVING 100 CALORIES
AT BREAKFAST SAVES
YOU 12 MINUTES ON
THE TREADMILL.

BREAKFAST

Start your day right by saving 100+ calories at breakfast! You've heard it before, but it's not a myth: Breakfast is the most important meal of the day. Research shows that eating a healthy breakfast helps you focus, concentrate, and—most importantly— eat less throughout the day. So even when you're pressed for time, the goal is to eat a better breakfast every day, whether you are cooking at home or eating on the go.

PANCAKES

Classic and universally appealing, pancakes are a breakfast staple. But it's all too easy to overdo it on syrup and butter. Get the same satisfying sweetness with fewer calories—just by thinking more creatively about your toppings.

lose it!
203
CALORIES SAVED

✗ Skip It
The 3-Stack Pancake Stack

Three 6-inch pancakes simply topped with butter (1 tablespoon) and a drizzle of maple syrup (¼ cup) seem reasonable for a meal, right? Nope. The calories in this no-brainer breakfast pile up.

582 calories, 9.6g sat fat, 636mg sodium

✓ Choose It
Crunchy Creamy Pancake Stack

Instead of butter and a heavy pour of syrup, top three 6-inch pancakes with rich, creamy fat-free Greek yogurt (1 tablespoon), crunchy chopped pecans (1 tablespoon), and a bit of maple syrup (1 tablespoon) for a satisfying breakfast with a contrast of textures.

379 calories, 2.7g sat fat, 532mg sodium

 NUTRITION ALERT *A Fruitful Addition*

Topping pancakes with fruit gives you an extra shot of a variety of vitamins, minerals, and disease-fighting antioxidants. Fruit adds sweetness so you only need a touch of maple syrup (1 tablespoon). Berries are also one of the best sources of compounds called polyphenols, which can help reduce your risk of cancer and heart disease.

WAFFLES

Waffles are easy to prepare and open to endless interpretations. Keep it hearty, but healthy, by incorporating whole grains. Or substitute fruit and a dusting of powdered sugar as a topping instead of syrup.

lose it!
389
CALORIES SAVED

✘ *Skip It*
Two-Waffle Stack with Butter

Two waffles topped with butter (1 tablespoon), syrup (¼ cup), and a hefty sprinkling of walnuts (2 tablespoons) is the stuff of a traditional weekend breakfast, but the calories can quickly add up with all those delicious toppings.

729 calories, 12.2g sat fat, 539mg sodium

✔ *Choose It*
Whole-Grain Waffle Stack

Substitute half of the all-purpose flour with whole-wheat flour in your waffle batter to bump up the fiber and whole-grain content, and then top your 2-waffle stack with 1 tablespoon reduced-sugar orange marmalade and 1 tablespoon fat-free whipped topping for refreshing sweetness.

340 calories, 4g sat fat, 428mg sodium

FROZEN WAFFLES

Toaster waffles can be an easy grab-and-go breakfast option and choosing a whole-grain version will help you get ahead on your daily fiber goal of 25-38 grams. One waffle should have less than 100 calories.

✖ *Skip It*

Syrup

Syrup is a calorie-dense food that's mostly sugar, so a little adds up: ¼ cup of maple syrup runs 210 calories. Instead, keep to a drizzle of lite syrup (1 table-spoon: 25 calories) or swap the syrup for fruit.

285 calories, 0g sat fat, 275mg sodium

SHOP SMART

Choose Healthy

Pick whole-wheat or multigrain frozen waffles with minimal added sugars (5g or less), like Van's™ or Kashi®. And look at the ingredients list to make sure whole grains or whole-grain flour is listed first.

✔ *Choose It*
Berries & Browned Butter

1 whole-grain toaster waffle + ²/₃ cup sliced strawberries tossed in 1 teaspoon brown sugar + 2 teaspoons browned butter + 2 tablespoons fresh basil leaves + 1 tablespoon toasted sliced almonds

239 calories, 5g sat fat, 109mg sodium

lose it!
46
CALORIES SAVED

✔ *Choose It* Skinny Elvis

1 whole-grain toaster waffle + ¹/₃ cup sliced bananas + 2 teaspoons creamy peanut butter + 1 center-cut bacon slice, crumbled + 1 teaspoon honey

239 calories, 2.2g sat fat, 290mg sodium

lose it!
46
CALORIES SAVED

✔ *Choose It*
Peaches & Cream

1 whole-grain toaster waffle + ¹/₄ cup vanilla light ice cream, softened + ²/₃ cup sliced peaches + Dash of cinnamon + 1 ¹/₂ tablespoons chopped pecans, toasted + 1 tablespoon fresh mint leaves

240 calories, 1.6g sat fat, 128mg sodium

lose it!
45
CALORIES SAVED

✔ *Choose It* Poached Egg & Avocado

1 whole-grain toaster waffle + 3 tablespoon thinly sliced avocado + 1 large poached egg + ¹/₂ ounce slivered prosciutto + 1 tablespoon chopped fresh cilantro + ¹/₄ cup chopped tomato

233 calories, 2.6g sat fat, 392mg sodium

lose it!
52
CALORIES SAVED

FRENCH TOAST

French toast is a favorite for more relaxed weekend breakfasts. This recipe gives you a healthy base to use for any bread and topping combination you like.

French Toast

ACTIVE 6 MINUTES | TOTAL 14 MINUTES

- **2 large eggs**
- **⅔ cup fat-free milk**
- **¼ teaspoon ground cinnamon**
- **1 teaspoon vanilla extract**
- **6 (1 to 1½-ounce) slices bread**

PREPARATION

Combine eggs, milk, cinnamon, and vanilla in a shallow bowl, stirring with a whisk until blended. Dip bread slices, 1 at a time, in egg mixture, turning to coat both sides. Heat a large nonstick skillet over medium-high heat. Add 3 coated bread slices; cook 2 minutes on each side or until lightly browned. Remove from pan. Repeat procedure with remaining coated bread slices. Serves 3 (serving size: 2 slices)

Per serving: 250 calories, 1.6g sat fat, 359mg sodium

 NUTRITION ALERT *Go for Whole Grains*

Whole-wheat bread has more fiber than white bread, so you'll feel fuller longer and eat less. Plus, it helps you get your fill of whole grains. Research has found that eating whole grains can help lower your risk of heart disease, diabetes, and colon cancer.

 +  +

541
CALORIES

✗ *Skip It* Classic French Toast Combo

White bread Texas toast (2 [1.4-ounce] slices) + one-third of egg mixture (from recipe)
+ ¹⁄₄ cup maple syrup + 1 tablespoon whipped cream
541 calories, 2.5g sat fat, 484mg sodium, 0.1g fiber

 +  +

lose it!
91
CALORIES
SAVED

✔ *Choose It* Banana-Chocolate Delight

Challah (2 [1-ounce] slices) + one-third of egg mixture (from recipe) + 1 tablespoon Nutella
+ 1 medium banana, sliced
450 calories, 3.5g sat fat, 368mg sodium, 3.7g fiber

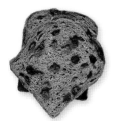 +  +

lose it!
188
CALORIES
SAVED

✔ *Choose It* Fruit & Nut

Cinnamon-raisin bread (2 [1-ounce] slices) + one-third of egg mixture (from recipe)
+ 1 tablespoon low-sugar raspberry preserves + 1 tablespoon peanut butter
353 calories, 2.6g sat fat, 358mg sodium, 3.1g fiber

COLD CEREAL

A bowl of milk and cereal is a speedy morning meal, but it can also be a calorie and sugar bomb if you don't choose carefully. Check out your best picks for 1 cup of cereal.

lose it!
286
CALORIES SAVED

✗ Skip It
Low-fat Granola & Fat-free Milk
(1 cup granola with ³/₄ cup fat-free milk)
442 calories

✔ Choose It
Low-fat Granola & Fat-free Greek Yogurt
(¹/₄ cup granola with ¹/₂ cup fat-free Greek yogurt)
156 calories

 SHOP SMART *Sugar Shocker*

Cereals are typically low in fat but high in sugar. Read the Nutrition Facts Panel carefully. One serving of a healthy cereal should:
- Be relatively low in sugar (10g or less).
- Be high in fiber (at least 3g).
- Contain at least one serving of whole grains (16g).
- Be free of artificial colors and dyes.

 RIGHT-SIZE-IT *Measure It*

Avoid large bowls (which beg to be filled) and use a measuring cup to keep portions in check until you're able to eyeball the right amount easily. Since cereals look different in the bowl, re-measure if you switch cereals. Some cereals, like granola, have way more calories by volume than others, so you may need to use a different measuring cup.

✗ *Skip It*
Cocoa Puffs®
(1 cup)
133 calories

✗ *Skip It*
Frosted Mini-Wheats®
(1 cup)
190 calories

✗ *Skip It*
Cracklin' Oat Bran®
(1 cup)
267 calories

lose it!
45
CALORIES
SAVED

✓ *Choose It*
Kix®
(1 cup)
88 calories

Bonus: *This swap saves you (and your kids) 11g sugar per cup!*

lose it!
70
CALORIES
SAVED

✓ *Choose It*
Barbara's Puffins®
(1 cup)
120 calories

lose it!
127
CALORIES
SAVED

✓ *Choose It*
Kashi GoLean®
(1 cup)
140 calories

Bonus: *Kashi cereal also boasts 13g protein, which means you won't be hungry an hour later.*

OATMEAL

Oatmeal is a naturally healthy choice. A hot bowl of oatmeal prepared from ¹/₂ cup dry oats and water offers a hearty base that's open to many topping variations. It clocks in at 150 calories and offers 4g of filling fiber and 5g of satiating protein.

NUTRITION ALERT *Steel-cut or Instant*

Having oatmeal every day is one of the easiest ways to get whole-grain, fiber-rich goodness. Whether you prefer steel-cut, rolled, or instant, you still get the same nutritional benefits. Just watch out for the added sugar and fat in prepackaged flavored oats.

✖ *Skip It*

Classic Oatmeal Topping

Think beyond the classic oatmeal topping of 2 tablespoons heavy cream, 1 tablespoon brown sugar, and 1 tablespoon chopped walnuts.

204 calories, 13.5g sat fat, 15mg sodium

✔ *Choose It* Fresh Apple & Honey

½ cup chopped fresh apple + 1 tablespoon honey

96 calories, 0g sat fat, 1mg sodium

lose it!
108
CALORIES SAVED

✔ *Choose It*

Peanut Butter & Chocolate

2 teaspoons peanut butter + 1 teaspoon chocolate syrup

83 calories, 0.7g sat fat, 43mg sodium

lose it!
121
CALORIES SAVED

✔ *Choose It* Berry Crunch

½ cup berries + 1 tablespoon sliced almonds

81 calories, 0.3g sat fat, 1mg sodium

lose it!
123
CALORIES SAVED

BREADS

What would your a.m. meal be without bread? But supersized bagels can contain more than 300 calories and 400mg sodium. Remember: Large bagels should have 250 calories or less; English muffins should have 130 calories or less; and bread should have 70 to 90 calories per slice.

RIGHT-SIZE-IT
Cream Cheese

Deli-counter prepared bagels and cream cheese usually pack in 2 tablespoons of cream cheese and 5.6g sat fat! You can switch to a low-fat version OR use a moderate 1 tablespoon of the regular kind to save on calories and fat.

lose it!

248
CALORIES
SAVED

✘ Skip It
Bagel, Lox, Cream Cheese

1 large poppy seed bagel with lox, capers, dill, and cream cheese

473 calories, 6.9g sat fat, 1,132mg sodium

✔ Choose It
Pumpernickel, Lox, Cream Cheese

2 (1-ounce) slices pumpernickel bread with lox, capers, dill, and 1 tablespoon cream cheese

225 calories, 3.3g sat fat, 966mg sodium

✖ *Skip It*
Cheese Bagel & Cream Cheese
Asiago cheese bagel with 2 tablespoons cream cheese

489 calories, 12.6g sat fat, 913mg sodium

✖ *Skip It*
Plain Bagel & Reduced-fat Cream Cheese
Plain bagel with 2 tablespoons reduced-fat cream cheese

370 calories, 3.5g sat fat, 670mg sodium

✖ *Skip It*
White Toast & Butter
2 (1-ounce) slices white-bread toast with 2 tablespoons butter

408 calories, 14.7g sat fat, 204mg sodium

lose it!
171
CALORIES
SAVED

lose it!
129
CALORIES
SAVED

lose it!
261
CALORIES
SAVED

✔ *Choose It*
Plain Bagel, Cream Cheese, Jam
3 ¹/₂-inch bagel with 1 tablespoon cream cheese and 1 tablespoon fruit jam

318 calories, 1.5g sat fat, 381mg sodium

✔ *Choose It*
Whole-wheat English Muffin, Peanut Butter, Strawberries
Whole-wheat English muffin with 1 tablespoon peanut butter and 2 tablespoons fresh strawberry slices

241 calories, 1.2g sat fat, 300mg sodium

✔ *Choose It*
Whole-wheat Toast, Provolone, Tomato
1 (1-ounce) slice whole-wheat toast with 1 thin slice provolone (melted) and 2 slices tomatoes

147 calories, 3.7g sat fat, 261mg sodium

TOAST

It's the easiest way to start the morning. The bread you use—and what you top it with—makes all the difference not only in calorie and fat count, but also in whether you'll be hungry an hour later! Try these carb-protein combos so you'll be sure to stay full until lunch.

✗ Skip It

Buttered Toast

The basic breakfast of 2 thick-cut slices of white bread with 2 pats of butter is pretty much devoid of any meaningful nutrients. You're primarily getting carbs and fat—which is no way to start the day.

377 calories, 14.6g sat fat, 614mg sodium

 SHOP SMART *Label Lingo*

As you're browsing the bread aisle, it can be hard to distinguish a healthy slice from a not-so-healthy slice thanks to the myriad health claims on labels. Watch out for these three red flags, which are signs that you're better off leaving that bread on the shelf:

MADE WITH WHOLE GRAINS. This means that the bread contains a blend of whole-wheat flour and another type—probably a not-as-nutritious flour. While it may be a step up from white bread, it's still not your best choice.

ENRICHED FLOUR. When breads are enriched, that means the flour has been processed, which removes most of the vitamins and minerals, and some of the nutrients (only five by law) have been added back in. So you're probably missing out on dozens of nutrients or more—including fiber.

BLEACHED FLOUR. Bleaching adds chemicals to breads while also destroying the pigments in the flour, which are beta-carotene that your body converts to vitamin A.

✔ **Choose It** Cheddar & Apple

1 slice cinnamon-raisin bread + 3/4 ounce shredded sharp cheddar cheese, melted + thinly sliced Granny Smith apple

180 calories, 4.5g sat fat, 237mg sodium

lose it!
197
CALORIES
SAVED

✔ **Choose It** Green Eggs & Ham

1 slice toasted ciabatta + 1 slice Canadian bacon + 1 soft-boiled egg + thinly sliced fresh basil sprinkled on top

200 calories, 2.6g sat fat, 499mg sodium

lose it!
177
CALORIES
SAVED

✔ **Choose It** Italian Style

1 slice toasted sourdough bread + 1 teaspoon olive oil, 1/4 cup canned white beans, 1 minced garlic clove, 1/4 teaspoon crushed red pepper heated on medium + fresh rosemary and parsley sprinkled on top

179 calories, 0.7g sat fat, 168mg sodium

lose it!
198
CALORIES
SAVED

✔ **Choose It** Ricotta-Pistachio Treat

1 slice toasted whole-grain bread + 2 tablespoons part-skim ricotta cheese + 1 teaspoon olive oil + 1 tablespoon crushed dry-roasted pistachios

176 calories, 2.6g sat fat, 137mg sodium

lose it!
201
CALORIES
SAVED

PASTRIES

You can satisfy your sweet tooth at breakfast without ruining your diet for the day. Store-bought muffins and pastries are often loaded with calories and fat (there's a reason they leave grease marks on a napkin). But you can find equally delicious— and more nutritious—options with some creative thinking.

lose it!
190
CALORIES SAVED

✖ *Skip It*
Large Bran Muffin
420 calories, 2g sat fat, 613mg sodium

✔ *Choose It*
Raisin Bran & Fat-free Milk
1 cup cereal with ¹/₂ cup fat-free milk
230 calories, 0.3 g sat fat, 302mg sodium

Bonus: This choice boasts 8g of fiber!

✖ *Skip It*

Cinnamon Roll

515 calories, 5g sat fat,
425mg sodium

✖ *Skip It*

Chocolate Croissant

560 calories, 16g sat fat,
330mg sodium

✖ *Skip It*

Large Blueberry Muffin

(5.5 ounces)

613 calories, 5.5g sat fat,
544mg sodium

lose it!
309
CALORIES SAVED

✔ *Choose It*

Toasted Raisin Bread & Cinnamon

*2 slices toasted raisin bread
with 1 tablespoon reduced-fat
cream cheese and sprinkled with
1 teaspoon each powdered sugar
and cinnamon*

206 calories, 1.8g sat fat,
260mg sodium

lose it!
369
CALORIES SAVED

✔ *Choose It*

French Bread, Nutella, & Fruit

*1 slice crusty French bread with 1
tablespoon chocolate-hazelnut
spread, fresh orange segments,
and a sprinkle of sea salt*

191 calories, 1.8g sat fat,
312mg sodium

lose it!
223
CALORIES SAVED

✔ *Choose It*

Moderately-sized Blueberry Muffin

(3.5 ounces)

390 calories, 3.5g sat fat,
346mg sodium

OMELET

Eggs are an excellent way to start the day: One egg has 13 essential nutrients, including folate, iron, B12, and protein—making eggs a filling, energizing choice. An omelet can be a low-calorie and budget-friendly choice; it all depends on how you make it.

✗ Skip It
The Classic Omelet

An egg-and-cheddar omelet (4 whole eggs and 3 [1-ounce] slices cheddar) with 2 slices thick-cut bacon seems like a pretty basic breakfast, but it can rack up the calories and saturated fat quickly—especially when whole milk, butter, and oil get tossed into the mix. Swapping out the cheese and cutting back on the eggs can save calories and fat. Tossing in veggies adds bulk, color, and flavor with minimal calories.

697 calories, 25.9g sat fat, 1,105mg sodium

🍎
NUTRITION ALERT

Egg Substitutes

Egg substitutes are a convenient and lower-calorie alternative to eggs because they're basically egg whites with food coloring added. They contain half the calories of eggs and no fat or cholesterol, but they do lack nutrients found in the yolk, including iron, vitamins D and B12, and riboflavin.

✔ *Choose It*
Western Omelet

Keep the cheesy flavor with this stuffed omelet, but subtract some of the calories with less cheese and lower-sodium ham.

ACTIVE 15 MINUTES | TOTAL 15 MINUTES

- 1 tablespoon water
- ⅛ teaspoon salt
- ⅛ teaspoon freshly ground black pepper
- 4 large eggs
- 1 tablespoon olive oil, divided
- ½ cup (1-inch) slices onion
- ⅓ cup (1-inch) slices red bell pepper
- ⅓ cup (1-inch) slices green bell pepper
- ¼ teaspoon chopped fresh thyme
- 2 ounces chopped 33%-less-sodium ham
- 1 ounce shredded Swiss cheese (about ¼ cup), divided

PREPARATION

1. Combine first 4 ingredients in a medium bowl, stirring with a whisk. Heat an 8-inch nonstick skillet over medium-high heat. Add 1 teaspoon oil to pan; swirl to coat. Stir in onion, bell peppers, thyme, and ham; sauté 4 minutes or until vegetables are crisp-tender. Remove vegetable mixture from pan; set aside. Clean pan.

2. Return pan to medium-high heat. Add 1 teaspoon oil to pan; swirl to coat. Add half of egg mixture to pan, tilting pan to spread evenly; cook 1 minute or until edges begin to set. Lift edge of omelet with a rubber spatula, tilting pan to roll uncooked egg mixture onto bottom of pan. Repeat procedure on opposite edge of omelet. Cook 1 minute or until center is just set. Sprinkle 2 tablespoons cheese evenly over omelet. Sprinkle half of vegetable mixture over cheese. Run the spatula around edges and under omelet to loosen it from pan; fold in half. Slide omelet onto a plate. Repeat procedure with remaining oil, egg mixture, cheese, and vegetable mixture. Serves 2 (serving size: 1 omelet)

Per serving: 331 calories, 6.5g sat fat, 608mg sodium

lose it!
366
CALORIES SAVED

BREAKFAST MEATS

Meats are a great source of protein for your morning meal, but can also be loaded with calories, fat, and sodium. Instead of the traditional favorites, you can work in turkey and ham. Why reserve them just for lunch?

lose it!
31
CALORIES
SAVED

✗ Skip It
Canadian Bacon
(2 slices)
76 calories, 1.1g sat fat, 634mg sodium

✔ Choose It
Ham
(2 thin slices)
45 calories, 0.4g sat fat, 500mg sodium

 NUTRITION ALERT *Center Cut vs. Regular Bacon*
Because it's cut closer to the bone, center-cut bacon has approximately 20% less saturated fat than regular—but you get the same satisfying flavor and crunch. Two slices of center-cut bacon have approximately 1g sat fat versus 2g for the same amount of regular bacon.

✘ *Skip It*
Turkey Breakfast Sausage
(3 ounces)
134 calories, 3g sat fat, 522mg sodium

✘ *Skip It*
Turkey Sausage Links
(2 links)
110 calories, 2g sat fat, 410mg sodium

✘ *Skip It*
Pork Sausage Links
(3 links)
260 calories, 6g sat fat, 580mg sodium

lose it!
94
CALORIES SAVED

✔ *Choose It*
Center-cut Bacon
(2 slices)
40 calories, 1g sat fat, 173mg sodium

lose it!
70
CALORIES SAVED

✔ *Choose It*
Turkey Bacon
(2 slices)
40 calories, 0.5g sat fat, 220mg sodium

lose it!
150
CALORIES SAVED

✔ *Choose It*
Pork Sausage Patties
(2 patties)
110 calories, 1.5g sat fat, 420mg sodium

BURGER KING®

Burger King is all about the breakfast sandwich on a croissant. However, this means you have a little less latitude with what you choose to go between the bread since a croissant itself can be pretty high in calories and fat. But you can still change up the meat-cheese combo.

lose it!
130
CALORIES SAVED

✘ *Skip It*
Sausage, Egg, and Cheese Croissan'wich®

The buttery, flakey croissant sure tastes good, but you've already got two super-high fat fillers in the sausage and cheese. So, at 180 calories and 3g sat fat, the croissant just unnecessarily piles on the greasiness.

500 calories, 12g sat fat, 930mg sodium

✔ *Choose It*
Bacon, Egg, and Cheese Croissan'wich

This sandwich is still pretty salty, but the amount of bacon included only accounts for 30 calories, 1g sat fat, and 110mg sodium. So you can get your salty meat fix for less.

370 calories, 9g sat fat, 770mg sodium

ORDER SMART AT BURGER KING

• **BETTER BREAKFAST CHOICES** Want something sweet? Instead of a giant cinnamon roll, go for the lower-calorie 3-Piece French Toast Sticks. Three strips with 1-ounce syrup provide 350 calories, 11g fat, and 2g sat fat. And it is also fairly low in sodium at 275mg per serving. Wash it down with fat-free milk to add an additional protein and calcium boost. The BK Breakfast Muffin Sandwich Egg and Cheese is not low in sodium at 830mg, but with 260 calories and 4g sat fat, it is the best breakfast sandwich choice on the menu.

• **BEWARE THE COMBO MEAL** At 250 calories extra, even the small side of hash browns (which are included in any meal) don't do you any favors. Instead, order your breakfast sandwich à la carte and avoid the fried temptation.

• **PORTION CONTROL** When it comes to the breakfast burritos at Burger King, you're better off having the two smaller Sausage Breakfast Burritos (620 calories, 14g sat fat, 1,640mg sodium) rather than the Southwestern Breakfast Burrito Meal (850 calories, 16.5g sat fat, 2,070mg sodium). With two items, you'll simply feel like you're eating more!

• **TRY A KIDS' MEAL** A reasonable, filling breakfast of oatmeal and apple slices, the Oatmeal Kids' Meal is pretty healthy at 170 calories, 1.5g sat fat, and 260mg sodium. You can even add a bottle of low-fat chocolate milk for 160 calories and 1.5g sat fat and up the protein content without breaking your calorie bank for breakfast.

 NUTRITION ALERT *That Has How Many Calories?!*
The Burger King Ultimate Breakfast Platter really lives up to its name: You get tons of food (pancakes, biscuit, hash browns, eggs, and sausage). But it's the ultimate fat, salt, and calorie bomb! At a whopping 1,420 calories, 29g sat fat, and 3,020mg sodium, you're eating a hefty chunk of calories and more than your *daily* sodium allotment at one meal.

DENNY'S®

An all-around favorite, Denny's has so many dishes to choose from that it's easy to go right—or wrong. It's not hard to spot the calorie, fat, and sodium bombs—there's usually way too much food on the plate. Don't come crazy-hungry or your eyes may be bigger than your stomach!

lose it!
30
CALORIES SAVED

✘ Skip It
Texas Prime Rib and Egg Sandwich
820 calories, 18g sat fat, 1,750mg sodium

✔ Choose It
Country Fried Steak with Eggs
790 calories, 15g sat fat, 1,940mg sodium

NUTRITION ALERT
What the What?! Calorie Shockers

It's all too easy to eat a day's worth (or more!) of calories, sat fat, and sodium in one sitting. Order these four dishes at your own risk:

- The Grand Slamwich® with hash browns:
  1,340 calories, 28g sat fat, 3,390mg sodium
- Meat-Lovers Omelette with hash browns:
  1,020 calories, 23g sat fat, 2,490mg sodium
- Lumberjack Slam®: **1,000 calories, 17g sat fat, 3,010mg sodium**
- Bacon Avocado Burrito with hash browns:
  1,050 calories, 20g sat fat, 2,400mg sodium

✘ *Skip It*
Banana Pecan Pancake Breakfast
750 calories, 2g sat fat, 1,590mg sodium

✘ *Skip It*
Santa Fe Skillet
710 calories, 15g sat fat, 1,490mg sodium

✘ *Skip It*
Sausage Slam®
2 sausage links, hash browns, and 2 buttermilk pancakes

830 calories, 13g sat fat, 2,100mg sodium

lose it!
160
CALORIES SAVED

✔ *Choose It*
Blueberry Pancake Breakfast
590 calories, 7g sat fat, 1,410mg sodium

lose it!
370
CALORIES SAVED

✔ *Choose It*
Fit Fare® Veggie Skillet
340 calories, 2g sat fat, 1,360mg sodium

Bonus: You could even go with 2 real eggs and still come in under 450 calories.

lose it!
440
CALORIES SAVED

✔ *Choose It*
Fit Slam®
2 egg whites scrambled with tomatoes and spinach, turkey bacon, toasted English muffin with jam, and fresh fruit

390 calories, 2g sat fat, 890mg sodium

DUNKIN' DONUTS®

Dunkin' Donuts has way more than donuts these days with lots of breakfast sandwiches, bagels, and muffins. They're even offering a fried egg and bacon sandwich on a glazed donut—which, surprisingly, isn't as high in calories as you might think at 380 per sandwich.

lose it!
70
CALORIES SAVED

✖ Skip It
Big 'n' Toasted®
530 calories, 10g sat fat, 1,360mg sodium

✔ Choose It
Bacon, Egg, and Cheese on a Bagel
460 calories, 4.5g sat fat, 1,200mg sodium

NUTRITION ALERT *Bagel vs. Doughnut*

At Dunkin' Donuts, believe it or not, the donut is often a better choice than their bagels, which all come in at 300 calories or more. Lower-calorie donut options include: Bavarian Kreme (270 calories) and Plain Glazed (260 calories).

ORDER SMART *Muffins*

Almost all the muffins at Dunkin' Donuts are significantly lower in calories than the Coffee Cake Muffin (at right)—with the exception of the Chocolate Chip Muffin which clocks in with 550 calories, 6g sat fat, and 470mg sodium.

✘ *Skip It*
Cinnamon Raisin Bagel Twist with 1 tablespoon cream cheese

350 calories, 0g sat fat, 510mg sodium

✘ *Skip It*
Coffee Cake Muffin

590 calories, 8g sat fat, 480mg sodium

✘ *Skip It*
Sausage, Egg, and Cheese on a Croissant

650 calories, 18g sat fat, 1,250mg sodium

lose it!
80
CALORIES SAVED

✔ *Choose It*
Apple 'n' Spice Donut

270 calories, 6g sat fat, 350mg sodium

lose it!
130
CALORIES SAVED

✔ *Choose It*
Blueberry Muffin

460 calories, 3g sat fat, 450mg sodium

lose it!
390
CALORIES SAVED

✔ *Choose It*
Egg and Sausage Wake-Up Wrap®

260 calories, 7g sat fat, 680mg sodium

Bonus: You can opt to have your sandwich on a biscuit or English muffin, both of which are lower in calories than the croissant.

IHOP®

IHOP is famous for its dessert-inspired pancake dishes, and who can resist concoctions called Tiramisu, Red Velvet, Jelly Donut, and Banana Graham Nut—all topped with whipped cream and drizzled with a sweet sauce. But, many of IHOP's breakfast entrées have such high calorie, fat, and sugar content, you might as well be eating a big slice of chocolate cake.

lose it!
300
CALORIES SAVED

✗ *Skip It*
Cinn-a-Stack® Pancakes

With the Cinn-a-Stack Pancakes, you're basically eating one giant cinnamon bun with a pretty hefty calorie load. Four buttermilk pancakes are layered with cinnamon roll filling, cream cheese icing, and whipped cream, which helps take this dish over the edge not only in calories and fat, but also in sugar, carbohydrates (109g), and sodium—and that doesn't include bacon or sausage!

900 calories, 10g sat fat, 2,250mg sodium

✔ *Choose It*
Whole Wheat Pancakes with Blueberries

These are the healthier pancake option on the menu, and you still get 4 pancakes and a blueberry topping sprinkled with powdered sugar—plus a dose of whole grains and 10g of filling fiber.

600 calories, 3g sat fat, 1,600mg sodium

ORDER SMART AT IHOP

· **BETTER BREAKFAST CHOICES** While the Harvest Grain 'n Nut® Pancakes may sound like the healthiest of IHOP's regular pancake options since they're made with grains, oats, almonds, and English walnuts (and have slightly lower sodium), they do have more calories than you may have bargained for. The best classic pancake choice is a short stack of three Original Buttermilk Pancakes (470 calories, 5g sat fat) or Whole Wheat Pancakes with Bananas (570 calories, 3g sat fat).

· **PORTION CONTROL** Ask for a half portion (two pancakes instead of four) and have them pack up the other two to take home before they bring your dish out. The pancakes and French toast are so filling, you can easily feel satisfied—not stuffed—with just two. Plus, you'll have breakfast for the next morning.

· **SIMPLE & FIT** Thankfully IHOP has made it easier for diet-conscious restaurant-goers to make smart choices. Their Simple & Fit menu offers entrées that are under 600 calories across all categories, including pancakes, waffles, omelets, and French toast. The servings are still generous, and you can put together combos (pancakes and eggs, French toast with bacon) so you still feel satisfied.

· **TOPPING SMARTS** It's too easy to overdo it on syrup and butter, but a little really does go a long way. Keep it to a 1-teaspoon "pat" of butter and 1 ounce of syrup. IHOP's syrups have between 100-110 calories per ounce, but their Sugar Free Syrup comes in at 15 calories an ounce. You can also ask to hold the butter or whipped topping.

 NUTRITION ALERT *That Has How Many Calories?!*

Beware of the combos at IHOP. Many contain an entire day's worth of calories and fat. Take the Country Fried Steak and Eggs entrée: It racks up 1,540 calories and 84g fat (23g sat fat). That's more than double the amount of fat you should eat daily! Other outrageous offenders: the Smokehouse Combo (1,330 calories, 28g sat fat), T-Bone Steak and Eggs (1,200 calories, 23g sat fat) and the Biscuits and Gravy Combo (1,380 calories, 31g to 34g sat fat, depending on the gravy you choose).

MCDONALD'S®

When you're grabbing a quick a.m. meal, there are lots of good options to consider at McDonald's. But be careful: What sounds like the healthiest choice just may not be the lowest in fat and calories. And some seemingly unhealthy options actually don't do that much damage.

 ✘ Skip It
Cinnamon Melts®
460 calories, 9g sat fat, 370mg sodium

lose it!
310
CALORIES SAVED

✔ Choose It
Fruit 'N' Yogurt Parfait
150 calories, 1g sat fat, 70mg sodium

🍎 NUTRITION ALERT
Skip the Breakfast Combo

Combine pancakes, eggs, and sausage and you're asking for trouble. None of the McDonald's "big" breakfasts come in under 700 calories. If you're dying for their hash browns (which are delicious), you're better off pairing one (150 calories, 1.5g sat fat, 310mg sodium) with an Egg White Delight McMuffin.

🥪 ORDER SMART *McMuffins*

Mickey-D's Egg McMuffin® is a healthy standby at 300 calories, and they now offer quite a few breakfast sandwiches on an English muffin, which are all pretty reasonable: Their Sausage McMuffin with Cheese runs 370 calories, 8g sat fat, 780mg sodium, and the Egg White Delight McMuffin (which includes a slice of Canadian bacon and white cheddar) is 250 calories, 3g sat fat, 800mg sodium.

✖ *Skip It*
Bacon, Egg, and Cheese Bagel

620 calories, 11g sat fat, 1,480mg sodium

✖ *Skip It*
Hotcakes

hotcakes with syrup and one pat of whipped margarine

570 calories, 3.5g sat fat, 660mg sodium

✖ *Skip It*
Sausage, Egg, and Cheese McGriddles®

550 calories, 12g sat fat, 1,320mg sodium

lose it!
160
CALORIES SAVED

✔ *Choose It*
Bacon, Egg, and Cheese Biscuit

460 calories, 13g sat fat, 1,300mg sodium

Bonus: The bagel is the deal-breaker here due to sheer size and heft. The biscuit will certainly have a richer, more buttery flavor but with fewer calories.

lose it!
280
CALORIES SAVED

✔ *Choose It*
Fruit & Maple Oatmeal

290 calories, 1.5g sat fat, 160mg sodium

lose it!
250
CALORIES SAVED

✔ *Choose It*
Sausage Burrito

300 calories, 7g sat fat, 790mg sodium

Bonus: For basically the same ingredients—sausage, scrambled egg, cheese—plus a kick of veggies, you slash the calories and sodium by more than half by nixing the pancake-like "bread."

PANERA BREAD®

Ordering a better-for-you breakfast is pretty easy at Panera since they have tons of options. Many dishes feature eggs and breakfast meats so you can eat the energizing combo of protein and carbs.

lose it!
100
CALORIES SAVED

✗ Skip It
Asiago Cheese Bagel with Bacon
610 calories, 13g sat fat, 1,350mg sodium

✔ Choose It
Bacon, Egg, and Cheese on Ciabatta
510 calories, 10g sat fat, 1,170mg sodium

 NUTRITION ALERT *Yogurt Delight*

One healthier option at Panera is the Strawberry Granola Yogurt Parfait (310 calories, 4.5g sat fat, 100mg sodium). The granola is house-made and is a nutty blend of toasted coconut, oats, pecans, honey, maple syrup, and brown sugar. It sounds fattening, but each component is portioned out just right in the parfait.

 ORDER SMART *The Hidden Menu*

Panera's "hidden menu" has some healthy options worth considering, most notably their power breakfast bowls, which are like little breakfast salads. Try the Power Breakfast Egg Bowl with Steak, which includes avocados and tomatoes (270 calories, 5g sat fat, 440mg sodium) and the Power Breakfast Egg White Bowl with Roasted Turkey, which also features roasted red pepper strips and baby spinach (170 calories, 0.5g sat fat, 500mg sodium).

✗ *Skip It*
French Toast Bagel with Sausage, Egg, and Cheese

670 calories, 14g sat fat, 1,280mg sodium

✗ *Skip It*
Sweet Onion and Poppy Seed Bagel with Steak

630 calories, 8g sat fat, 950mg sodium

✗ *Skip It*
Pecan Roll Pastry

740 calories, 12g sat fat, 320mg sodium

lose it!
110 CALORIES SAVED

✓ *Choose It*
Sausage and Gouda Baked Egg Soufflé

560 calories, 19g sat fat, 890mg sodium

lose it!
290 CALORIES SAVED

✓ *Choose It*
Breakfast Power with Ham on Whole-Grain Miche

340 calories, 7g sat fat, 920mg sodium

lose it!
400 CALORIES SAVED

✓ *Choose It*
Steel-Cut Oatmeal with Strawberries and Pecans

340 calories, 1.5g sat fat, 160mg sodium

Bonus: You get the same sweet and nutty flavor for less fat and fewer calories plus a hefty dose of filling fiber (9g) from the steel-cut oats and fruit.

STARBUCKS®

You can go with the usual breakfast fare of muffins, scones, and breakfast sandwiches, but there are plenty of healthier options to choose from. Consider the protein box, which has a distinctly a.m. feel with an egg, apple, and multigrain muesli bread.

lose it!
150
CALORIES SAVED

✖ Skip It
Sausage and Cheddar Breakfast Sandwich
500 calories, 9g sat fat, 920mg sodium

✔ Choose It
Bacon and Gouda Breakfast Sandwich
350 calories, 7g sat fat, 820mg sodium

 NUTRITION ALERT *Try the Oatmeal*
Many fast-food places include oatmeal on their breakfast menus, and Starbucks is no exception. But Starbucks doesn't simply heat up an instant packet: Their oatmeal is made from rolled oats and boasts 4g fiber plus 5g protein. Even better, the toppings are portion-controlled in small-sized packets.

 ORDER SMART *Veggie Isn't Always Better*
Cutting out meat doesn't necessarily mean cutting down calories. At Starbucks, the Chicken Sausage Breakfast Wrap (300 calories, 3g sat fat, 700mg sodium) comes in pretty close to the Spinach and Feta Breakfast Wrap (290 calories, 3.5g sat fat, 830mg sodium). Often more cheese (and calories and fat) is added to make up for less meat.

✗ *Skip It*

Blueberry Scone

420 calories, 10g sat fat, 510mg sodium

✗ *Skip It*

Cheese Danish

320 calories, 9g sat fat, 390mg sodium

lose it!
100
CALORIES
SAVED

✓ *Choose It*

Blueberry Yogurt Muffin with Honey

320 calories, 3g sat fat, 260mg sodium

lose it!
20
CALORIES
SAVED

✓ *Choose It*

Chonga Bagel

(topped with cheddar cheese, poppy seeds, and onion)

300 calories, 2g sat fat, 530mg sodium

SUBWAY®

Flatbreads, English muffins, and 6-inch sub rolls at Subway all offer solid starting points for a healthy breakfast sub. Use any of these three options as a base; opt for wheat or honey oat bread if you go with the sub roll—they offer the most fiber.

✗ *Skip It*

Egg, Cheddar, Tomato, Mayo, Olives, Avocado, Bacon

620 calories, 10g sat fat, 1,090mg sodium

 NUTRITION ALERT *Know Your Breads*

Before putting together your breakfast sandwich, check out how the different breads stack up:
- 6-inch Italian white sub: 200 calories, 1g fiber
- 6-inch 9-grain wheat bread: 210 calories, 4g fiber
- 6-inch Parmesan oregano bread: 220 calories, 2g fiber
- 6-inch flatbread: 220 calories, 2g fiber

 ORDER SMART *Egg Whites*

For any of these combos, you can swap in egg white for eggs and automatically save 40 calories and 2g sat fat.

lose it!
250
CALORIES
SAVED

✔ **Choose It** Cheese and Greens with Bacon

Provolone + egg white + spinach + bacon + avocado = 370 calories, 4.5g sat fat, 1,090mg sodium

lose it!
180
CALORIES
SAVED

✔ **Choose It** Egg, Swiss, and Bacon

Swiss cheese + egg + tomato + bacon = 440 calories, 6g sat fat, 950mg sodium

lose it!
300
CALORIES
SAVED

✔ **Choose It** Tomato and Cheese

Cheddar cheese + egg white + tomato = 320 calories, 3g sat fat, 900mg sodium

▶KEEP LUNCH LIGHT.
LIMIT POURS OF HEAVY,
CALORIE-RICH CONDIMENTS
AND DRESSINGS.

LUNCH

There's a reason that, in some countries, lunch—not dinner—is the biggest meal of the day. Just as crucial as breakfast in terms of giving you long-lasting energy, lunch should be a balanced combo of healthy carbs, protein, and a bit of "good" fat to help you power through the afternoon.

BUILD A BETTER SANDWICH

Sandwiches are the super-easy, speedy lunch option, and they can be healthy, too, if you choose the right lean meats and cheeses. Pile on delicious vegetables (and fruit!), and you'll get an extra dose of vitamins, minerals, and filling fiber.

✖ *Skip It*
Stuffed Turkey Sandwich

An onion roll piled high with deli turkey and cheddar cheese, plus a hefty smear of mayo, also piles on the calories.

511 calories, 9.1g sat fat, 1,602mg sodium

 RIGHT-SIZE-IT *Meat*

Deli sandwiches are often stacked tall with piles of deli meats, sometimes upwards of 6 ounces. The result: Extra calories and a hefty dose of sodium. To keep these numbers in check, use just 2 ounces of thinly sliced deli meat—thinly sliced meat will stack higher—and opt for lower-sodium versions when possible.

✔ Choose It Roast Beef with Pesto

2 slices 100% whole-wheat bread + 2 ounces lower-sodium roast beef + 1 ounce goat cheese +
1 tablespoon pesto = 399 calories, 8.6g sat fat, 629mg sodium

lose it!
112
CALORIES
SAVED

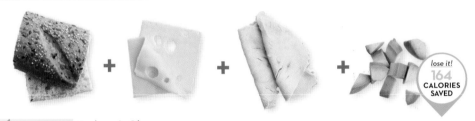

✔ Choose It Turkey & Cheese

Multigrain baguette + 1-ounce slice Swiss cheese + 2 ounces lower-sodium turkey + 2 tablespoons
chopped avocado = 347 calories, 5.6g sat fat, 693mg sodium

lose it!
164
CALORIES
SAVED

✔ Choose It Healthier Pastrami

2 slices rye bread + 2 ounces beef pastrami + 1 tablespoon canola mayo + 1 teaspoon mustard =
251 calories, 0.9g sat fat, 1,021mg sodium

lose it!
260
CALORIES
SAVED

SALAD SANDWICHES

These lunchtime staples sound healthy since their base ingredients—chicken, eggs, tuna—are ideal protein sources. But, when you pile on the mayo or use too many eggs, you might as well eat a hamburger. Opt for two slices of multi-grain bread (about 140 calories) and a lighter salad filling.

lose it!

219
CALORIES
SAVED

✘ *Skip It*
Classic Tuna Salad
With regular full-fat mayo and diced celery

1 cup: 400 calories, 4.5g sat fat, 559mg sodium

✔ *Choose It*
Mediterranean Tuna Salad
12-ounce can albacore tuna in water + ½ cup thinly sliced red onion + 2 thinly sliced celery stalks + 2 tablespoons chopped kalamata olives + 2½ tablespoons fresh lemon juice + 1 tablespoon olive oil + ¼ teaspoon black pepper + ⅛ teaspoon kosher salt

1 cup: 181 calories, 1g sat fat, 587mg sodium

✘ *Skip It*
Classic Egg Salad
With whole hard-cooked eggs and regular full-fat mayo
1 cup: 460 calories, 8g sat fat, 1,140mg sodium

✘ *Skip It*
Traditional Chicken Salad
With dark and light meat and regular full-fat mayo
1 cup: 640 calories, 6.5g sat fat, 473mg sodium

lose it!
90
CALORIES SAVED

✔ *Choose It*
Lightened Egg Salad
8 hard-cooked chopped egg whites + 6 hard-cooked chopped yolks + ¼ cup canola mayo + 3 tablespoons chopped green onions + 3 tablespoons reduced-fat sour cream + 2 teaspoons Dijon mustard + ½ teaspoon black pepper + ¼ teaspoon grated lemon rind
1 cup: 370 calories, 6.7g sat fat, 592mg sodium

lose it!
501
CALORIES SAVED

✔ *Choose It*
Avocado Chicken Salad
3 cups shredded cooked chicken breast + ¼ cup canola mayo + 2 tablespoons chopped fresh cilantro + ¼ teaspoon salt + ⅛ teaspoon black pepper + 1 cup cubed avocado
1 cup: 139 calories, 0.9g sat fat, 158mg sodium

CONDIMENTS

Condiments are key to adding flavor to a sandwich and can also contain healthy fats, antioxidants, vitamins, and minerals. For most though, you'll need to avoid slathering and keep portions in check to avoid going overboard on calories, saturated fat, and sodium.

✗ *Skip It*

Thousand Island Dressing

Creamy sauces add flavor and rich mouth-feel to an everyday turkey sandwich, but think beyond this favorite topper.

2 tablespoons:
120 calories, 1.5g sat fat, 310mg sodium

✔ Choose It

Mustard

Most mustards have no fat and sugar, and there are many varieties to choose from, including classic yellow mustard.

1 tablespoon: 9 calories, 0.5g sat fat, 168mg sodium

lose it!
111
CALORIES SAVED

✔ Choose It

Pesto

Olive oil and pine nuts mean lots of good fats and fewer calories than mayo.

1 tablespoon: 78 calories, 0.8g sat fat, 148 mg sodium

lose it!
42
CALORIES SAVED

✔ Choose It

Hummus

Great as a veggie dip but it's also delicious as a sandwich spread. Made from chickpeas, hummus offers a small dose of fiber (0.5g) in just 1 tablespoon.

1 tablespoon: 25 calories, 0g sat fat, 57mg sodium

lose it!
95
CALORIES SAVED

✔ Choose It

Canola Mayonnaise

Mayo made with canola oil has the same amount of calories and sodium per tablespoon as real mayo, but the benefit comes in the boost in healthy fats. You also can use light mayo (50 calories, 0.8g sat fat, and a slightly higher sodium of 130mg).

1 tablespoon: 100 calories, 1g sat fat, 90mg sodium

lose it!
20
CALORIES SAVED

✔ Choose It

Barbecue Sauce

The thicker the barbecue sauce, the more calories it contains. Many thinner sauces still pack loads of flavor.

1 tablespoon: 30 calories, 0g sat fat, 120mg sodium

lose it!
90
CALORIES SAVED

✔ Choose It

Tapenade

This tangy mixture is low in calories and full of healthy fat, but the briny olives pack in sodium. Just a dab of this highly flavorful spread will do.

1 tablespoon: 45 calories, 1g sat fat, 150mg sodium

lose it!
75
CALORIES SAVED

BAKED POTATOES

Potatoes can be a complete—and compact—meal customized with assorted toppings to your heart's desire. One medium spud has 160 calories and 3.8g fiber.

 RIGHT-SIZE-IT *Spud Size*

A whopper potato can pack more calories than a 6-ounce sirloin, so to give your toppings the most acreage, stick with a medium-sized spud. Check out how small to extra-large spuds stack up:

- Extra-large (4½ to 6 inches) = 512 calories
- Large (3 to 4¼ inches) = 325 calories
- Medium (2¼ to 3¼ inches) = 160-190 calories
- Small (1¾ to 2½ inches) = 150 calories

✘ *Skip It*
Traditional Baked Potato Toppers
Toppings like 1 tablespoon butter, ¼ cup sour cream, and ¼ cup shredded cheddar cheese don't make the most of the potato's nutritional potential.

336 calories, 20.3g fat, 367mg sodium

✔ **Choose It** Classic Combo Lightened
2 tablespoons reduced-fat sour-cream + 1 tablespoon shredded reduced-fat cheddar cheese + 1 strip center-cut bacon + 1 tablespoon sliced green onions

100 calories, 4.5g sat fat, 210mg sodium

lose it!
236
CALORIES SAVED

✔ **Choose It** BBQ Chicken
⅓ cup rotisserie chicken breast + 1 tablespoon barbecue sauce + 1 tablespoon sliced green onions

83 calories, 0.4g sat fat, 277mg sodium

lose it!
253
CALORIES SAVED

✔ **Choose It** Chili Style
¼ cup canned kidney beans + 2 tablespoons sliced red onion + 2 tablespoons shredded reduced-fat cheddar

100 calories, 1.7g sat, 292mg sodium

lose it!
236
CALORIES SAVED

SALADS

These traditional salad stand-bys are notoriously delicious and creamy, mostly because they contain lots of high-calorie and high-fat foods—bacon, blue cheese, croutons, oh my! The key is to adjust the amount of these types of ingredients and make lighter versions of the dressings.

lose it!
328
CALORIES SAVED

✘ *Skip It*
Traditional Chicken Caesar

Topped with croutons, Parmesan cheese, chicken, and creamy Caesar dressing

600 calories, 8g sat fat, 1,180mg sodium

✔ *Choose It*
Lightened Chicken Caesar

2 cups romaine lettuce + ½ cup cubed toasted French bread + ⅔ cup sliced cooked chicken + 1 tablespoon grated Parmesan cheese; topped with a dressing made with a dash of black pepper + ½ tablespoon white wine vinegar + ½ tablespoon olive oil + ¼ teaspoon bottled minced garlic + ¼ teaspoon Dijon mustard + ⅛ teaspoon anchovy paste

272 calories, 2.3g sat fat, 322mg sodium

✘ *Skip It*
Taco Salad with Beef

Ground beef, olives, shredded cheese, and tomatoes served in a fried taco shell

780 calories, 10g sat fat, 1,380mg sodium

✘ *Skip It*
Classic Chef Salad

Romaine lettuce with diced deli turkey, grape tomatoes, croutons, hard-boiled eggs, shredded cheddar cheese, and Ranch dressing

774 calories, 15.4g sat fat, 2,364mg sodium

lose it!
410
CALORIES SAVED

✔ *Choose It*
Lightened Taco Salad with Beef

Cook 3 ounces ground sirloin and ¼ cup chopped onion in a nonstick skillet over medium-high heat until browned. Add ¼ cup fresh salsa and ¼ cup fresh corn; bring to a boil. Stir in 1 tablespoon chopped fresh cilantro. Layer 12 baked tortilla chips with 1 cup shredded romaine lettuce, meat mixture, ½ cup chopped plum tomato, ¼ cup reduced-fat shredded sharp cheddar cheese, and 1 tablespoon chopped green onions.

370 calories, 6.2g sat fat, 620mg sodium

lose it!
371
CALORIES SAVED

✔ *Choose It*
Lightened Chef Salad

2 cups chopped romaine lettuce + ¾ cup shredded skinless, boneless rotisserie chicken breast + ⅓ cup halved grape tomatoes + 1 hard-boiled egg + ¼ cup crumbled blue cheese + 2 tablespoons balsamic vinaigrette

403 calories, 8.4g sat fat, 618mg sodium

COBB SALAD

Cobb Salad is one of America's most popular salads, but the traditional recipe is chockfull of bacon, seasoned chicken, and mounds of cheese, avocado, and hard-boiled egg, which can sometimes be too much of a good thing.

✗ *Skip It*
Classic Cobb Salad

Romaine topped with chicken, avocado, hard-boiled eggs, blue cheese, chopped tomato, green onions, bacon, and Ranch dressing.

1,150 calories, 24g sat fat, and 1,960mg sodium

RIGHT-SIZE-IT
Dressing

Restaurant and fast-food salads are often drowning in dressing, which can add 300+ calories to an otherwise virtuous meal. Always ask for salad dressing on the side, and then add one or two tablespoons yourself.

lose it!
887
CALORIES SAVED

✔ *Choose It*
Lightened Chicken Cobb Salad

This keeps the components of the traditional version, but cutting back on the oil-based dressing and the avocado immediately brings the fat and calories down.

ACTIVE 30 MINUTES | TOTAL 48 MINUTES

> Cooking spray
> 1½ pounds skinless, boneless chicken breast cutlets
> ¼ teaspoon salt
> ¼ teaspoon freshly ground black pepper
> 8 cups mixed greens
> 1 cup cherry tomatoes, halved
> ⅓ cup diced peeled avocado
> 2 tablespoons sliced green onions
> ⅓ cup fat-free Italian dressing
> 2 tablespoons crumbled blue cheese
> 1 bacon slice, cooked and crumbled

PREPARATION

1. Heat a large nonstick skillet over medium-high heat. Coat pan with cooking spray. Sprinkle chicken with salt and pepper. Add chicken to pan; cook 5 minutes on each side or until done. Cut into ½-inch slices.

2. Combine greens, tomatoes, avocado, and onions in a large bowl. Drizzle greens mixture with dressing; toss gently to coat. Arrange about 2 cups greens mixture on each of 4 salad plates. Top each serving with 4 ounces chicken, 1½ teaspoons cheese, and about ½ teaspoon bacon. Serves 4 (serving size: approximately 2 cups)

Per serving: 263 Calories, 2.4g sat fat, 606mg sodium

GREEN SALADS

Mixed greens as the base of a good-for-you bowl of salad can provide two or more servings of vegetables and lots of lean protein and healthy fats. But salads can easily go awry—and pack just as many calories and fat as a cheeseburger—if you don't choose your toppings wisely. Start with 2 cups of greens, a tablespoon of vinaigrette, and top with one of these 100-calorie combos.

 **NUTRITION ALERT**

Salad Dressing

Dressings add tons of flavor to salads, but they can also pack on calories, fat, and sodium if you pour too much. An oil and vinegar–based dressing is usually your best bet, but you can pick a creamier option if you keep the serving to 1 to 1½ tablespoons. You can also choose a lower-fat alternative of your favorite—look for those that have 40 calories or less and no more than 0.5g saturated fat per tablespoon. Here's the rundown of how 2-tablespoon servings of salad dressings clock-in:

- Blue cheese: 172 calories
- Ranch: 140 calories
- French: 140 calories
- Creamy Parmesan: 130 calories
- Caesar: 120 calories
- Dijon mustard: 100 calories
- Italian vinaigrette: 100 calories
- Light Ranch: 80 calories

✘ Skip It
Traditional Green Salad Toppers

Classic salad toppings like 2 ounces diced turkey, ½ cup shredded cheddar cheese, and ½ cup croutons add up.

383 calories, 13.5g sat fat, 1,062mg sodium

✔ Choose It Greek

¼ cup sliced red bell pepper + 2 tablespoons crumbled feta cheese + ¼ cup chopped fresh cucumber + 2 tablespoons chopped kalamata olives

100 calories, 2.8g sat fat, 466mg sodium

lose it!
283 CALORIES SAVED

✔ Choose It Classic Caprese

2 plum tomatoes, sliced + 2 tablespoons chopped fresh basil + 1 ounce fresh mozzarella, sliced

100 calories, 4g sat fat, 23mg sodium

lose it!
283 CALORIES SAVED

✔ Choose It Nuts, Berries & Cheese

1 tablespoon crumbled blue cheese + 1 tablespoon sweetened dried cranberries + 1 tablespoon chopped toasted walnuts

100 calories, 2g sat fat, 118mg sodium

lose it!
283 CALORIES SAVED

GRAIN SALADS

Grain-based salads are a healthy alternative to pasta salad. You get the same hearty base but with more protein and fiber. We've based these picks on quinoa, which cooks quickly (about 20 minutes) and is whole grain and gluten free. Use this easy base recipe: Start with ²/₃ cup cooked quinoa (148 calories, 5.4g protein, 3.5g fiber), and add your favorite combos. You can also sub in farro (133 calories, 3.4g protein, 2.3g fiber per ²/₃ cup), barley (129 calories, 2.4g protein, 4g fiber) or bulgur (101 calories, 3.7g protein, 5.5g fiber). Cook on Sunday, chill, and eat over the next few days. A perfect portable lunch!

✗ Skip It
Feta & Olives

An overload of calorie-heavy toppings is where these salads can go awry. ¹/₄ cup feta cheese + ¹/₄ cup olives + 2 tablespoons olive oil

376 calories, 9.8g sat fat, 666mg sodium

✔ *Choose It* Roots, Shoots & Greens

¼ cup roasted sweet potato cubes + ½ cup fresh baby spinach + 1 tablespoon chopped toasted pecans + 1 tablespoon thinly sliced green onions

117 calories, 0.5g sat fat, 44mg sodium

lose it!
259
CALORIES SAVED

✔ *Choose It* Heirlooms & Avocado

½ cup heirloom cherry tomatoes + ¼ cup sliced avocado + 3 tablespoons fresh cilantro + ¾ teaspoon extra-virgin olive oil

105 calories, 1.3g sat fat, 6mg sodium

lose it!
271
CALORIES SAVED

✔ *Choose It* The Nutty Moroccan

3 tablespoons cooked chickpeas + ¼ cup julienned fresh carrot + 2 tablespoons toasted pine nuts + 2 tablespoons chopped fresh parsley

165 calories, 0.9g sat fat, 129mg sodium

lose it!
211
CALORIES SAVED

✔ *Choose It* Rise & Shine

¼ cup fresh blueberries + 1 tablespoon chopped toasted walnuts + 2 teaspoons brown sugar + ¼ teaspoon cinnamon

105 calories, 0.5g sat fat, 3mg sodium

lose it!
271
CALORIES SAVED

CANNED SOUP

A satisfying meal in a bowl, soup can be an easy way to meet your daily vegetable servings. But, many common soup ingredients can carry a hefty calorie load, and canned soups can also be very high in sodium.

lose it!
80
CALORIES SAVED

✘ Skip It
Progresso® Traditional
New England Clam Chowder
(1 cup)
180 calories, 2g sat fat, 860mg sodium

✔ Choose It
Progresso Light New England
Clam Chowder
(1 cup)
100 calories, 0.5g sat fat, 690mg sodium

 SHOP SMART *Soup Rules*

Look for soups with the fewest ingredients. Ideally a 1-cup serving of canned soup or stew should have 250 calories or less, 5g of sat fat or less, and less than 800mg of sodium.

✖ Skip It

Campbell's® Chunky Grilled
Steak with Beans Chili

(1 cup)

200 calories, 1g sat fat, 870mg sodium

✖ Skip It

Campbell's Split Pea with
Ham and Bacon Soup

(1 cup)

360 calories, 1g sat fat, 1,700mg sodium

lose it!
60
CALORIES
SAVED

✔ Choose It

Campbell's Sirloin Burger
with Country Vegetables

(1 cup)

140 calories, 2.5g sat fat, 790mg sodium

lose it!
140
CALORIES
SAVED

✔ Choose It

Amy's® Indian Golden
Lentil Soup

(1 cup)

220 calories, 1g sat fat, 680mg sodium

AU BON PAIN®

Au Bon Pain has numerous options for healthy eating. You can search their menu for dishes that meet your dietary preferences, including high protein, high fiber, low sodium, and low saturated fat. And browse their Petit Plates menu for items that are 310 calories or less.

lose it!
260
CALORIES SAVED

✘ *Skip It*

Red Beans, Italian Sausage, and Rice Soup *(large)*

410 calories, 3g sat fat, 1,660mg sodium

✔ *Choose It*

Chicken Noodle Soup *(large)*

150 calories, 1g sat fat, 1,290mg sodium

 ORDER SMART *Pick "Petit Plates"*

ABP offers great little dishes called Petit Plates, which are ideal alone or paired with a soup. They're all between 200 to 310 calories and include just-right portions of delicious cheeses like Brie and cheddar (no low-fat versions here!) or greens and protein.

 NUTRITION ALERT *Hot & Cold Lunch Bar*

Some ABP locations have a lunch bar, which features a spread of tasty dishes including pasta salad, green beans, eggplant Parmesan, meatballs, even lasagna and meatloaf. This can be a great way to create a smorgasbord lunch, but be cautious about portion sizes. One ounce of anything doesn't do too much damage. To avoid going overboard, choose one protein (chicken, meatballs, meatloaf), one carbohydrate (potatoes, pasta, rice), and one veggie.

✖ *Skip It*
Black Forest Ham and Cheddar Sandwich

640 calories, 7g sat fat, 1,720mg sodium

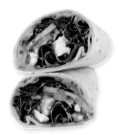

✖ *Skip It*
Mediterranean Wrap

620 calories, 11g sat fat, 1,401mg sodium

✖ *Skip It*
Mac and Cheese *(large)*

710 calories, 24g sat fat, 1,560mg sodium

lose it!
130 CALORIES SAVED

✔ *Choose It*
Black Angus Roast Beef and Cheddar Sandwich

510 calories, 8g sat fat, 1,740mg sodium

lose it!
120 CALORIES SAVED

✔ *Choose It*
Napa Chicken with Avocado Wrap

500 calories, 6g sat fat, 1,700mg sodium

lose it!
350 CALORIES SAVED

✔ *Choose It*
Split Pea with Ham *(large)*

360 calories, 1g sat fat, 1,710mg sodium

CHICK-FIL-A®

Just because a fast-food place is all about chicken doesn't mean everything on the menu is healthy. Also, don't let the word "salad" in the title of a dish fool you: Some Chick-fil-A salads and salad sandwiches pack a hefty calorie and fat load.

lose it!
130
CALORIES SAVED

 ✗ *Skip It*
Spicy Chicken Sandwich Deluxe
570 calories, 8g sat fat, 1,790mg sodium

 ✓ *Choose It*
Classic Chicken Sandwich on a bun with a pickle
440 calories, 4g sat fat, 1,390mg sodium

NUTRITION ALERT *Side Standoff*

Chick-fil-A has lots of delicious sides, but be careful. The portions look small but they're big in the calorie and fat department: The cup of coleslaw has 360 calories and 5g sat fat, and the chicken salad cup has 360 calories and 5g sat fat.

ORDER SMART *Nutritious Nuggets*

The nuggets at Chick-fil-A are a good way to get your fried chicken fix. Go with the kids' meal version: 6 chicken nuggets have just 200 calories, 2g sat fat, and 790mg sodium; 2 chicken strips have 240 calories, 3g sat fat, and 660mg sodium. They even have grilled chicken nuggets: With a side of honey mustard sauce, they run 145 calories, 0g sat fat, and 550mg sodium.

✗ *Skip It*
Cobb Salad with honey sesame dressing

600 calories, 9g sat fat, 1,980mg sodium

✗ *Skip It*
Chicken Salad Sandwich

500 calories, 4g sat fat, 1,120mg sodium

✗ *Skip It*
Chicken Salad Cup with a side salad

440 calories, 8g sat fat, 1,230mg sodium

lose it!
170
CALORIES
SAVED

lose it!
160
CALORIES
SAVED

lose it!
190
CALORIES
SAVED

✔ *Choose It*
Asian Salad with fat-free honey mustard dressing

430 calories, 3g sat fat, 1,450mg sodium

✔ *Choose It*
Grilled Chicken Cool Wrap®
(without avocado-lime dressing)

340 calories, 5g sat fat, 900mg sodium

✔ *Choose It*
Grilled Market Salad with a fruit cup

250 calories, 2g sat fat, 570mg sodium

CHIPOTLE® BURRITO

Burritos are a great compact meal, and Chipotle has tons of low-cal veggie sides and fillers to choose from. The flour tortilla base has a fair amount of calories (300) to start. The meat fillings (chicken, steak, carnitas, barbacoa) all have 165 to 220 calories, but the other add-ons are where the calorie pile-up can begin.

✖ Skip It
Fully-loaded

Chicken + brown rice + black beans + cheese + roasted chili-corn salsa + sour cream + guacamole + shredded lettuce

1,300 calories, 19g sat fat, 2,305mg sodium

✔ Choose It Beans, Cheese & Vegetables

Chicken + pinto beans + cheese + fajita vegetables + shredded lettuce

720 calories, 9g sat fat, 1,660mg sodium

lose it!
580
CALORIES SAVED

✔ Choose It Cheese & Vegetables

Chicken + cheese + fajita veggies + shredded lettuce

605 calories, 9g sat fat, 1,360mg sodium

lose it!
695
CALORIES SAVED

✔ Choose It Veg-Heavy

Chicken + tomato salsa + fajita vegetables + shredded lettuce

525 calories, 4g sat fat, 1,670mg sodium

lose it!
775
CALORIES SAVED

CHIPOTLE® SALAD

Salad can definitely be a healthy choice at Chipotle since it comes in a regular bowl instead of an edible fried taco shell. You're better off skipping rice (185 calories for white, 200 calories for brown) and not ordering chips and fresh tomato salsa on the side since that will add 590 calories, 3.5g sat fat, and 920mg sodium.

✖ *Skip It*
Fully-loaded Salad

Shredded lettuce + carnitas + white rice + black beans + guacamole + cheese + vinaigrette

1,105 calories, 18.5g sat fat, 2,510mg sodium

✔ *Choose It*
Dressed Black Bean Salad

Shredded lettuce + barbacoa + black beans + cheese + vinaigrette

665 calories, 12g sat fat, 1,835mg sodium

lose it!
440
CALORIES SAVED

✔ *Choose It* Chicken Salsa Salad

Shredded lettuce + chicken + roasted chili-corn salsa + honey vinaigrette

540 calories, 7.5g sat fat, 1,495mg sodium

lose it!
565
CALORIES SAVED

✔ *Choose It* Veg-Heavy Steak Salad

Shredded lettuce + steak + fajita veggies + fresh tomato salsa + guacamole

440 calories, 5g sat fat, 1,325mg sodium

lose it!
665
CALORIES SAVED

KFC®

All fried chicken is not created equal: Some KFC recipes are decidedly more caloric than others. So when you're putting together a bucket, consider how the chicken is fried. In general, KFC's original recipe chicken tends to be lower in calories and saturated fat.

lose it!
200
CALORIES SAVED

✘ Skip It

Spicy Crispy Chicken Breast

520 calories, 5g sat fat, 1,220mg sodium

✔ Choose It

Original Recipe® Chicken Breast

320 calories, 5g sat fat, 1,130mg sodium

NUTRITION ALERT *Skip the Skin*

You can request any original recipe piece of chicken without skin or breading, which automatically slashes the calories, saturated fat, and sodium content. A chicken breast prepared this way has a reasonable 130 calories, 0.5g sat, and 520mg sodium.

ORDER SMART *Dipping Sauces*

If you're splurging on fried chicken, you don't always need the sauces, but they can amp up the flavor of grilled chicken. The two best-bet sauces are sweet and sour (45 calories, 0g fat, 95mg sodium) and honey barbecue (40 calories, 0g fat, 310mg sodium). The creamy buffalo sauce starts to inch up at 70 calories, 7g fat, 510mg sodium, and the honey mustard clocks in at 120 calories, 10g fat, 110mg sodium.

✗ *Skip It*
Extra Crispy™ Whole Wing

210 calories, 2.5g sat fat, 490mg sodium

✗ *Skip It*
Potato Wedges

290 calories, 2.5g sat fat, 810mg sodium

✗ *Skip It*
BBQ Baked Beans

210 calories, 0.5g sat fat, 780mg sodium

lose it!
70
CALORIES SAVED

✔ *Choose It*
Original Recipe Whole Wing

140 calories, 1.5g sat fat, 450mg sodium

lose it!
170
CALORIES SAVED

✔ *Choose It*
Mashed Potatoes and Gravy

120 calories, 1g sat fat, 530mg sodium

Bonus: *If you skip the gravy, this side drops another 30 calories.*

lose it!
110
CALORIES SAVED

✔ *Choose It*
Sweet Kernel Corn

100 calories, 0.5g sat fat, 0mg sodium

MCDONALD'S®

Aside from hamburgers, McDonald's has a large variety of sandwiches, many of which aren't too bad calorie-wise. The real damage can happen when you order a meal complete with a soda and French fries. The best advice: Skip the combos and order items separately.

lose it!
150
CALORIES SAVED

✘ Skip It
Premium Crispy Chicken Sandwich
510 calories, 3.5g sat fat, 990mg sodium

✔ Choose It
McChicken®
360 calories, 3g sat fat, 800mg sodium

RIGHT-SIZE-IT *French Fries*

If you must indulge, size matters. Go small to save yourself extra gym time. Here's the breakdown:
- Large = 510 calories, 3.5g sat fat, 290mg sodium
- Medium = 340 calories, 2.5g sat fat, 190mg sodium
- Small = 230 calories, 1.5 g sat fat, 130mg sodium

ORDER SMART *Satisfying Sides*

A small side salad or a packet of apple slices can bulk up your meal for minimal calories. Plus, you'll increase your intake of fruits and vegetables. A side salad (greens with tomatoes and carrots) is only 20 calories and 0g of fat, and one packet of apple slices is 15 calories and has over 100% of your recommended daily intake for vitamin C.

✗ *Skip It*
10-Piece Chicken McNuggets®
470 calories, 5g sat fat, 900mg sodium

✗ *Skip It*
Premium Grilled McWrap® Chicken & Bacon
480 calories, 7g sat fat, 1,370mg sodium

✗ *Skip It*
Premium Crispy Chicken Club Sandwich
670 calories, 9g sat fat, 1,410mg sodium

lose it!
225
CALORIES SAVED

✔ *Choose It*
4-Piece Chicken McNuggets and Side Salad with low-fat balsamic vinaigrette
245 calories, 4.5g sat fat, 790mg sodium

lose it!
100
CALORIES SAVED

✔ *Choose It*
Premium Grilled McWrap Sweet Chili Chicken
380 calories, 3g sat fat, 1,090mg sodium

lose it!
240
CALORIES SAVED

✔ *Choose It*
Southern Style Crispy Chicken Sandwich
430 calories, 3g sat fat, 910mg sodium

PANERA BREAD®

Panera has many good options for a healthy lunch on the go, and the effort to rid its menu of artificial food additives is reassuring. Ask for their "hidden" menu items like the Power Mediterranean Chicken Salad or the Power Chicken Hummus Bowl for some of the healthiest choices.

lose it!
130
CALORIES SAVED

✘ Skip It
Fuji Apple Chicken Salad
550 calories, 7g sat fat, 620mg sodium

✔ Choose It
Asian Sesame Chicken Salad
420 calories, 3.5g sat fat, 500mg sodium

 NUTRITION ALERT *Beware the Panini*
Even the lowest-calorie option—Smokehouse Turkey with Bacon on Three Cheese Miche—runs 720 calories, 12g sat fat, and 2,590mg sodium.

 ORDER SMART *Try the Kids' Menu*
Seriously! The options are deliciously basic—PB&J, grilled cheese, ham, roast beef or turkey on white bread, and the portions are just right—even for an adult. Most items are 400 calories or under, too. (The exception is the small Mac & Cheese, which has 490 calories.) If you're worried about feeling satisfied, pair a kids' entrée with a small side salad.

✗ *Skip It*
Napa Almond Chicken Salad
on Sesame Semolina
700 calories, 4g sat fat, 1,190mg sodium

✗ *Skip It*
Sierra Turkey on Asiago Cheese
Focaccia
820 calories, 9g sat fat, 1,940mg sodium

lose it!
190
CALORIES
SAVED

✓ *Choose It*
Tuna Salad on Honey Wheat
510 calories, 4g sat fat, 1,150mg sodium

lose it!
390
CALORIES
SAVED

✓ *Choose It*
Smoked Turkey Breast on Country
Bread
430 calories, 1g sat fat, 1,790mg sodium

STARBUCKS®

You can get much more than your morning (or afternoon) cup of coffee at Starbucks these days, including a full spread for lunch. Their Bistro Boxes are a unique touch and a great healthy option.

lose it!
90
CALORIES SAVED

✖ Skip It
Egg Salad Sandwich
100 calories, 5g sat fat, 750mg sodium

100 calories, 5g sat fat, 750mg sodium
500 calories, 5g sat fat, 750mg sodium

✔ Choose It
Chicken Santa Fe Panini
410 calories, 6g sat fat, 930mg sodium

NUTRITION ALERT
Resist Check-Out Temptations

So you've done your homework and ordered the healthiest, lowest-calorie option. You're about to pay and you see...chocolate-covered berries, chocolate bars, packages of nuts. Just pay your bill and keep moving! Little extras are strategically placed near the cash register in hopes that you'll make an impulse decision to add another item to your purchase.

ORDER SMART *Build Your Own Meal*

The Chicken and Hummus Box (270 calories, 0g sat fat, 580mg sodium) makes a great base for a customized lunch. Pair it with a Seasonal Harvest Fruit Blend (90 calories, 0g sat fat, 0mg sodium) for a delicious and filling meal that offers 21g protein and 9g fiber.

✘ *Skip It*
Cheese & Fruit Box
480 calories, 10g sat fat, 470mg sodium

✘ *Skip It*
Chicken BLT Salad Sandwich
470 calories, 4.5g sat fat, 930mg sodium

✘ *Skip It*
Turkey Rustico Panini
480 calories, 6g sat fat, 1,120mg sodium

lose it!
100
CALORIES
SAVED

✔ *Choose It*
Protein Box
380 calories, 6g sat fat, 470mg sodium

Bonus: This platter offers a lot more variety for fewer calories: One egg, white cheddar cheese, honey peanut spread, multigrain muesli bread, apples, and grapes.

lose it!
110
CALORIES
SAVED

✔ *Choose It*
Zesty Chicken and Black Bean Salad Bowl
360 calories, 2.5g sat fat, 850mg sodium

lose it!
90
CALORIES
SAVED

✔ *Choose It*
Roasted Tomato and Mozzarella Panini
390 calories, 6g sat fat, 630mg sodium

SUBWAY®

In the grand scheme of fast-food joints, Subway is one of the healthiest of the bunch. They have eight basic 6-inch sandwiches that run 370 calories or less, and offer a variety of meats and healthy breads, including 9-grain wheat and honey oat, which are flavorful substitutes for plain white bread. Still, there are some options that save more calories, fat, and sodium than others.

lose it!
100
CALORIES SAVED

✘ Skip It
Italian BMT® *(6-inch)*
410 calories, 6g sat fat, 1,260mg sodium

✔ Choose It
Subway Club® *(6-inch)*
310 calories, 1.5g sat fat, 800mg sodium

Bonus: By opting for the club, you get three different meats—sliced turkey, lean roast beef, and Black Forest ham—for a reasonable amount of calories.

 NUTRITION ALERT

Make Your Sandwich into a Salad

Turn any 6-inch sub into a salad, and you'll easily cut 150 calories. Plus, you'll get more veggies. It's also another great way to get your craving for crunchy chips. When you cut the bread, have chips instead. Here's how two of the salads stack up against their sandwich counterparts:

- Big Philly Cheese Sandwich (500 calories, 9g sat fat, 1,280mg sodium) vs. Big Philly Cheese Salad (330 calories, 8g sat fat, 1,080mg sodium)
- Spicy Italian Sandwich (480 calories, 9g sat fat, 1,490mg sodium) vs. Spicy Italian Salad (310 calories, 8g sat fat, 1,280mg sodium)

✗ Skip It

Tuna *(6-inch)*

480 calories, 4g sat fat, 600mg sodium

✗ Skip It

Big Philly Cheesesteak *(6-inch)*

500 calories, 9g sat fat, 1,280mg sodium

✗ Skip It

Chicken & Bacon Ranch Salad with Ranch Dressing

510 calories, 11g sat fat, 1,050mg sodium

lose it!
110 CALORIES SAVED

✓ Choose It

Sweet Onion Chicken Teriyaki *(6-inch)*

370 calories, 1g sat fat, 770mg sodium

lose it!
120 CALORIES SAVED

✓ Choose It

Steak & Cheese *(6-inch)*

380 calories, 4.5g sat fat, 1,030mg sodium

lose it!
290 CALORIES SAVED

✓ Choose It

Oven-Roasted Chicken Chopped Salad with honey mustard dressing

220 calories, 0.5g sat fat, 600mg sodium

TACO BELL®

Taco Bell has changed up some of their tacos, burritos, and combo meals to reduce calories, fat, and sodium, but they still have plenty of heftier offerings filled with cheese, guacamole, and sour cream that you need to watch out for.

lose it!
220
CALORIES SAVED

✖ *Skip It*
Cheesy Gordita Crunch
490 calories, 10g sat fat, 830mg sodium

✔ *Choose It*
Chicken Gordita Supreme®
270 calories, 3.5g sat fat, 530mg sodium

NUTRITION ALERT *Cantina Power*

The Cantina Power items offer more than 20g protein and are 500 calories or less, but are they healthier? Keeping under 500 calories at lunch is good, but with 5-8g sat fat and 930-1,270mg sodium per item, there are better choices. And though protein is necessary, most Americans are already taking in much more than the recommended daily amount.

ORDER SMART AT TACO BELL

• **GO FRESCO** The Fresco menu features burritos and tacos at 350 calories or less. The Fresco Grilled Steak Soft Taco (150 calories, 1.5g sat fat, 440mg sodium) is the best choice and has a low sodium level. Or order any item on their regular menu "fresco" to swap out fillings like cheese, sour cream, guacamole for less-fattening pico de gallo salsa.

• **THINK 1:1:1** To keep calories in check, just follow a few general rules of thumb: Go with options that have only one or two creamy fillings like cheese, sour cream, guacamole, and special dressings; one protein (meat, chicken, or beans); and one carbohydrate (either a tortilla or rice).

• **SMARTER CHOICE** You're better off having two Chicken Soft Tacos (320 calories, 5g sat fat, 960mg sodium) than a Chicken Quesadilla (510 calories, 12g sat fat, 1,200mg sodium).

• **FOODS TO AVOID** Remember to look at a food's sodium count, which can affect blood pressure and heart health, as well as its calorie and fat amounts. Stay away from these overloaded items:

    Beef Smothered Burrito: 700 calories, 13g sat fat, 2,260mg sodium
    Steak XXL Grilled Stuft Burrito: 840 calories, 12g sat fat, 2,100mg sodium

 NUTRITION ALERT *Skip the Salads—Seriously!*
They might seem like a healthy choice, but the crispy tortilla bowl, white rice, and loads of cheese doom this dish from the start. None of the fiesta taco salads come in under 700 calories. The Fiesta Beef Taco Salad clocks in with the most at 780 calories; with steak, it's 740 calories; subbing in chicken only drops it to 730 calories.

WENDY'S®

What makes Wendy's different from all the other fast-food restaurants? Their baked potatoes and chili of course! Swap out fries for a spud or a hamburger for a small chili—or put them together for a hearty, delicious meal (see Order Smart below).

lose it!
120
CALORIES
SAVED

✘ *Skip It*
Crispy Chicken Sandwich
380 calories, 4g sat fat, 720mg sodium

✔ *Choose It*
6-Piece Spicy Chicken Nuggets
260 calories, 3.5g sat fat, 750mg sodium

NUTRITION ALERT *Croutons*

Their crunchy, bready deliciousness adds texture to salads, but they also add fat and calories. The croutons in the Spicy Chicken Caesar salad, for example, add 80 calories and 3g fat. Many fast-food restaurants offer croutons on the side—so always ask!

ORDER SMART *Consider a Baked Potato*

A Wendy's staple, a baked potato can be a healthy alternative to a meal or a side of French fries. That is, if you keep it simple. Skip the cheddar cheese sauce (150 calories, 8g sat fat, 480mg sodium) and ask for broccoli (15 calories, 0g sat fat, 15mg sodium) with one packet of reduced-fat sour cream (40 calories, 2g sat fat, 25mg sodium) and buttery spread (50 calories, 1g sat fat, 95mg sodium) on the side. The single-serve packets make portion control a no-brainer.

✘ *Skip It*

Chili Cheese Fries

520 calories, 9g sat fat, 1,070mg sodium

✘ *Skip It*

Spicy Chicken Caesar Salad

(full size)

780 calories, 16g sat fat, 1,650mg sodium

lose it!
30
CALORIES
SAVED

✔ *Choose It*

Small Chili and Baked Potato

(with 1 packet reduced-fat sour cream)

490 calories, 4g sat fat, 830mg sodium

lose it!
190
CALORIES
SAVED

✔ *Choose It*

Apple Pecan Chicken Salad

(full size)

590 calories, 8g sat fat, 1,330mg sodium

FOCUS ON YOUR FOOD, NOT THE TV OR SMART PHONE. RESEARCH SHOWS THAT DISTRACTED EATERS CONSUME MORE CALORIES.

DINNER

Top off your day by downsizing the last meal of the day. The more colorful your plate is, the better, since that means you're eating the widest variety of vitamins, minerals, and nutrients. To keep portions in check, use this visual as a guide: One fourth of your plate should be a whole grain (carbohydrate), one fourth lean protein, and half vegetables and/or greens.

BUILD A BETTER BURGER

Burgers can absolutely be a part of a healthy diet. A ¼-pound patty of lean ground sirloin and a hearty whole-grain bun start you out at 250 calories. Try finishing it off with one of these 100-calorie-or-less combinations.

✖ *Skip It*
Traditional Cheeseburger

2 slices cheddar cheese + 1 tablespoon mayo + 1 tablespoon ketchup + lettuce + 1 tomato slice

637 calories, 17.4g sat fat, 861mg sodium

NUTRITION ALERT
Lean and Leaner

When you're buying ground beef, pay attention to the percentages.
- Ground chuck is 80% lean, which means it's 20% fat.
- Ground round is 15% fat.
- Ground sirloin is 10% fat.

You may find meat that's simply labeled "lean ground beef," and that usually means it's 7% fat—and that's the leanest available.

✔ Choose It
All-American

2 teaspoons ketchup + 3 dill pickle chips + 1 thin slice sharp cheddar + green leaf lettuce + 1 tomato slice

84 calories, 2.6g sat fat, 483mg sodium

lose it!
303
CALORIES
SAVED

✔ Choose It
Avocado-Mango Tango

2 thin slices avocado + 2 tablespoons mango salsa + 1 tablespoon chopped fresh cilantro + 2 table-spoons shredded Monterey Jack cheese

79 calories, 2.8g sat fat, 162mg sodium

lose it!
308
CALORIES
SAVED

✔ Choose It
Caprese

1 ounce fresh buffalo mozzarella + ½ teaspoon extra-virgin olive oil + 2 heirloom tomato slices + 6 basil leaves

100 calories, 3.9g sat fat, 17mg sodium

lose it!
287
CALORIES
SAVED

✔ Choose It
Sun-Dried Summer

2 tablespoons chopped sun-dried tomatoes + ¼ cup fresh spinach + 1 ounce goat cheese

96 calories, 4.2g sat fat, 131mg sodium

lose it!
291
CALORIES
SAVED

BURGERS

They're as American as apple pie, but burgers can be so huge that you can barely bite into them. You can have a juicy, flavorful burger without breaking your calorie and fat budget. It's about choosing the right ground beef and making the patty a reasonable, but still satisfying, size.

lose it!
306
CALORIES SAVED

✗ *Skip It*
The Classic Bacon Cheeseburger

The typical bacon cheeseburger can be mammoth, with ⅓ pound (that's raw weight) of ground chuck (that's 20% fat), and then topped with all the classic favorites: sharp cheddar cheese, bacon, and all the standard toppings like mayo, ketchup, mustard, lettuce, tomato, and onion on a white hamburger bun.

807 calories, 23.4g sat fat, 905mg sodium

✔ *Choose It*
The Lighter Bacon Cheeseburger

Making a healthier burger doesn't mean sacrificing flavor. Opt for ground sirloin (at 10% fat) and make your patty ¼-pound. Top it with a slice of sharp cheddar and 2 slices of center-cut bacon. Add 2 teaspoons each of canola mayo and ketchup to add moisture. Keep the tomato, lettuce, and onion, but up the fiber by switching to a whole-wheat bun.

501 calories, 11.9g sat fat, 768mg sodium

STEAK

When you hear "steak" you might think "fatty," but certain cuts of steak are pretty lean and have less saturated fat than some cuts of chicken. Look for the leanest cuts with less visible fat (for example, tenderloin, flank steak, top sirloin). Serving size matters, too: Stick with 6 ounces or less.

lose it!
860
CALORIES SAVED

✘ *Skip It*
The 10-Ounce Ribeye Dinner

Ribeye is one of the fattier cuts of beef, with 15g saturated fat. And 10 ounces is a pretty hefty serving portion. Pairing the steak with mashed potatoes made with butter, whole milk, and sometimes cream can pile on additional calories. A typical steakhouse wedge salad really isn't much of a salad at all, with just a hunk of iceberg (the least nutritious) lettuce doused in blue cheese dressing.

1,269 calories, 32g sat fat, 2,525mg sodium

✔ *Choose It*
Flank Steak Dinner

Opting for lean flank steak and switching up the sides can save significant calories and saturated fat. Go for 6 ounces of grilled flank steak with ⅔ cup potato wedges seasoned with herbs and 1 tablespoon flavorful Parmesan cheese plus 2 cups spinach salad topped with ½ cup fresh vegetables and 1 tablespoon balsamic vinaigrette for a colorful and filling meal.

409 calories, 5.1g sat fat, 472mg sodium

FRIED CHICKEN

There are a few ways to lighten traditional fried chicken. Stick with chicken breasts to help cut down on saturated fat and replace the full-fat buttermilk with low-fat. This recipe makes a big dent in the calories, fat, and sodium but still delivers flavor and crunch.

✖ Skip It

Country Fried Chicken

Traditional country fried chicken recipes call for coating chicken in buttermilk, then flour and seasoning, and then deep-frying in oil (and sometimes bacon drippings) until browned and crispy. This recipe produces delicious results, but can add up to a pretty large nutritional load.

607 calories, 10.8g sat fat, 937mg sodium

 **NUTRITION ALERT** *Dark vs. Light*

Chicken is undoubtedly the go-to healthy protein. A lean, skinless chicken breast half contains 182 calories and 4g of fat (only 1.1g sat fat). It's a great source of protein in a convenient package. But there are some rules. **Rule #1:** Remove the skin. **Rule #2:** Know the difference between dark and light meat. Light, which includes the breast, is a healthier option because it contains about 50% less saturated fat than the dark thigh, leg, and wing meat. Don't ban dark meat from your diet—just keep portion sizes in check.

Walnut and Rosemary Oven-Fried Chicken

Instead of dark and light meat, stick with chicken breasts to help cut down on saturated fat and amp up the flavor with herbs. The panko gives this chicken its great color and crunch.

ACTIVE 12 MINUTES | TOTAL 25 MINUTES

¼ cup low-fat buttermilk

2 tablespoons Dijon mustard

4 (6-ounce) chicken cutlets

⅓ cup panko (Japanese breadcrumbs)

⅓ cup finely chopped walnuts

2 tablespoons freshly grated Parmigiano-Reggiano cheese

¾ teaspoon minced fresh rosemary

¼ teaspoon kosher salt

¼ teaspoon freshly ground black pepper

Cooking spray

Rosemary leaves (optional)

lose it!
315
CALORIES SAVED

PREPARATION

Preheat oven to 425°. Combine buttermilk and mustard in a shallow dish, stirring with a whisk. Add chicken to buttermilk mixture, turning to coat. Heat a small skillet over medium-high heat. Add panko to pan; cook 3 minutes or until golden, stirring frequently. Combine panko, nuts, and next 4 ingredients (through pepper) in a shallow dish. Remove chicken from buttermilk mixture; discard buttermilk mixture. Dredge chicken in panko mixture. Arrange a wire rack on a large baking sheet; coat rack with cooking spray. Arrange chicken on rack; coat chicken with cooking spray. Bake at 425° for 13 minutes or until chicken is done. Garnish with rosemary leaves, if desired. Serves 4 (serving size: 1 cutlet)

Per serving: 292 calories, 1.6g sat fat, 471mg sodium

CHICKEN FINGERS

Chicken fingers are one of the most popular finger foods for adults and kids alike. But most restaurants make them heavily battered and deep-fried, which can turn an otherwise healthy lean protein into a calorie and fat bomb.

✗ Skip It
Fried Chicken Fingers

At most restaurants and fast-food places, chicken fingers are strips of poultry dipped in a heavy batter, and then deep-fried for crunch. Toss in a creamy dipping sauce, and you add calories, salt, and sugar, too.

703 calories, 10.7g sat fat, 1,000mg sodium

NUTRITION ALERT *Chicken's Salty Secret*

Chicken that you buy in the supermarket is just chicken, plain and simple, right? Not necessarily. About one-third of fresh poultry in supermarkets has been enhanced with a mix of water, salt, and other additives—either by injection or high-pressure vacuum tumbling. Disclosure is required, but if you don't read the label carefully, the information is easy to miss. Check labels: Treated chicken will say something like "contains up to 15% chicken broth," and look for salt on the ingredients list. A truly natural chicken has no more than 70mg sodium per serving.

lose it!
329
CALORIES
SAVED

✔ *Choose It*
Pan-Fried Chicken Fingers

Instead of deep-fried, these chicken fingers are pan-fried in a small amount of canola oil.

ACTIVE 25 MINUTES | TOTAL 25 MINUTES

- ¼ cup all-purpose flour
- 1½ teaspoons freshly ground black pepper
- 1½ teaspoons paprika
- 2 large eggs, lightly beaten
- 1 tablespoon water
- 3 cups whole-grain flake cereal (such as Kashi 7-Grain Flakes), finely crushed (about 2½ cups)
- 1 pound chicken breast tenders
- ¼ teaspoon salt
- 1½ tablespoons canola oil

PREPARATION

Combine flour, black pepper, and paprika in a shallow dish. Combine eggs and 1 tablespoon water in another shallow dish. Place crushed cereal in another shallow dish. Sprinkle chicken evenly with salt. Working with 1 piece at a time, dredge chicken in flour mixture, dip in egg mixture, and dredge in cereal. Heat a large skillet over medium-high heat. Add oil to pan, swirling to coat. Add chicken pieces to pan; cook 2 minutes on each side or until done. Serves 4 (serving size: about 3 ounces chicken)

Per serving: 374 calories, 1.5g sat fat, 314mg sodium

STUFFED CHICKEN

Stuffed chicken breasts, like the traditional Chicken Cordon Bleu, are impressive looking and easier to prepare than you might think. You can stuff them up to a day ahead with one of these healthier ingredient combos, keep them refrigerated, and then simply cook and serve.

✗ Skip It
Chicken Cordon Bleu

This classic meal is certainly impressive on the plate, but since the chicken is stuffed with ham and cheese, breaded, deep-fried, and then topped with hollandaise sauce, the nutritional cost may be more than you bargained for.

1,166 calories, 30.8g sat fat, 2,234mg sodium

Start with 4 (6-ounce) chicken breasts. Sprinkle with ¼ teaspoon each salt and freshly ground black pepper. Heat a large oven-proof skillet over medium-high heat. Add 1 tablespoon canola oil to pan; swirl to coat. Add chicken; sauté 4 minutes. Turn chicken over, and transfer the pan to the oven. Bake at 350° for 12 minutes, and then let stand for 5 minutes. Drain.

✔ *Choose It*
Mushroom & Parmesan Stuffing

1 teaspoon olive oil + ½ cup chopped onion + 1 cup sliced mushrooms + 1 (10-ounce) package frozen chopped spinach + 2 tablespoons shredded Parmesan cheese + ½ teaspoon dried Italian seasoning + ¼ teaspoon salt + ¼ teaspoon freshly ground black pepper

263 calories, 1.4g sat fat, 968mg sodium

lose it!
903
CALORIES
SAVED

✔ *Choose It*
Pimiento Cheese Stuffing

1 slice cooked bacon, crumbled + ¾ cup shredded cheddar cheese + 2 tablespoons minced green onions + 1½ tablespoons diced pimientos + 1 tablespoon canola mayonnaise + 2 teaspoons fresh lemon juice + ½ teaspoon hot sauce + ½ teaspoon salt

299 calories, 5.8g sat fat, 606mg sodium

lose it!
867
CALORIES
SAVED

✔ *Choose It*
Almond & Cheese Stuffing

⅓ cup light garlic-and-herb spreadable cheese (such as Boursin light) + ¼ cup toasted slivered almonds, coarsely chopped + 3 tablespoons chopped fresh parsley

288 calories, 4.3g sat fat, 496mg sodium

lose it!
878
CALORIES
SAVED

✔ *Choose It*
Bacon & Goat Cheese Stuffing

2 tablespoons sliced green onions + 3 ounces goat cheese + 1 slice cooked bacon, crumbled

283 calories, 4.8g sat fat, 503mg sodium

lose it!
883
CALORIES
SAVED

FRIED FISH

Fish is the ultimate health food—it's a great source of lean protein. To get the most health benefits, experts recommend working fish into your diet twice a week. Nutritionally speaking, fresh and frozen are the same; for top-quality flash frozen, look for "frozen-at-sea" (FAS).

✖ Skip It
Deep-Fried Fish

Classic beer-battered deep-frying turns one of the most important building blocks of a healthy diet—fish—into a splurge meal.

423 calories,
2.4g sat fat,
779mg sodium

⬭ ORDER SMART *Menu Decoder*

When it comes to seafood dishes, these four words are code for "fried."

Basket: Fried food comes in a paper-lined basket to absorb the oil.
Strips: They're impossible to grill because they'd fall through the grates.
Chips: Always fried potatoes, so in other words, they're French fries.
Popcorn: As in shrimp. They're all too easy to eat by the handful.

NUTRITION ALERT

Watch Out for Mercury

Some fish and shellfish contain high levels of mercury that can inhibit brain development in fetuses and young children. Those with the highest level of mercury include shark, swordfish, king mackerel, and tilefish and should be avoided by pregnant women, women who may become pregnant, nursing mothers, and young children.

lose it!
127
CALORIES SAVED

✔ *Choose It*
Oven-Fried Catfish

The key to lightening up the fish? Light beer, cornmeal, no sugar, and no deep-fat-frying in the Dutch oven.

ACTIVE 7 MINUTES | TOTAL 52 MINUTES

½ cup light beer

½ cup hot sauce

4 (6-ounce) farm-raised catfish fillets

½ cup yellow cornmeal

2 tablespoons cornstarch

⅛ teaspoon salt

⅛ teaspoon freshly ground black pepper

Cooking spray

PREPARATION

Preheat oven to 450°. Combine first 3 ingredients in a large zip-top plastic bag; seal and marinate in refrigerator 30 minutes. Remove fish from bag; pat dry with paper towels. Discard marinade. Combine cornmeal, cornstarch, salt, and pepper in a shallow dish. Dredge fish in cornmeal mixture and lightly coat with cooking spray. Place on a baking sheet coated with cooking spray. Bake at 450° for 15 minutes or until the fish flakes easily when tested with a fork. Serves 4 (serving size: 1 fillet)

Per serving: 296 calories, 1.9g sat fat, 361mg sodium

BUILD A BETTER STIR-FRY

A stir-fry is a smart choice on many counts: Not only can you add 2 servings of veggies (or more) to your meal, it's also an easy way to make lean protein and whole grains the stars. Heat a wok or a large nonstick skillet over medium-high heat. Add the beef, chicken, shrimp, or tofu to the pan first to get a nice browned crust, and then add the vegetables and cook until browned and tender. Finish with the sauce, tossing to combine. A ½ cup of brown rice to serve alongside each of these stir-fries adds 108 calories.

✗ Skip It

Beef Sirloin Stir-Fry

Stir-frying up a combo of beef strips and broccoli with a sweetened peanut sauce can stir up a lot of calories.

**503 calories,
4.6g sat fat,
701mg sodium**

✔ **Choose It** Shrimp Stir-Fry

6 ounces raw shrimp + ½ cup sliced bell peppers + 1 cup snap peas + Ginger-Hoisin Sauce (1½ teaspoons minced green onions, 2 teaspoons rice wine vinegar, 1½ teaspoons lower-sodium soy sauce, 1 teaspoon peeled fresh ginger, ½ teaspoon honey, and 1 teaspoon hoisin sauce) = 260 calories, 0.8g sat fat, 694mg sodium

lose it!
243
CALORIES SAVED

✔ **Choose It** Chicken Stir-Fry

4 ounces cut-up chicken thigh + ½ cup sliced mushrooms + ½ cup shredded cabbage + ½ cup cooked snap peas + Coconut-Ginger Sauce (½ teaspoon minced peeled fresh ginger, 1 minced garlic clove, 1 teaspoon Sriracha, 2 teaspoons lower-sodium soy sauce, 1 teaspoon red curry paste, 2 tablespoons light coconut milk) = 217 calories, 2.3g sat fat, 657mg sodium

lose it!
286
CALORIES SAVED

✔ **Choose It** Tofu Stir-Fry

4 ounces extra-firm tofu + ½ cup green beans + ½ cup sliced carrots + ½ cup thinly sliced green onions + Teriyaki Sauce (1 tablespoon lower-sodium soy sauce, ½ teaspoon sugar, 1 teaspoon rice wine vinegar, ½ teaspoon minced peeled fresh ginger, ⅛ teaspoon crushed red pepper, 1 minced garlic clove, ¾ teaspoon cornstarch, 1 teaspoon water) = 197 calories, 0.7g sat fat, 652mg sodium

lose it!
306
CALORIES SAVED

PIZZA

Pizza is the perfect dinner: The right combination of crust and nutrient-packed ingredients—including fresh vegetables and lean protein—make a healthy meal-in-a-pie. Roll a 1-pound ball of refrigerated fresh pizza dough into a 14-inch base, and then top with tasty toppings that cater to your individual palate. Bake and divide by 8.

✗ *Skip It*
Meat Lover's Pizza

One slice of the classic pizza with a tomato sauce base topped with pepperoni, ground beef, bacon, and cheese takes you well on the way to a calorie convention.

390 calories, 8.1g sat fat, 928mg sodium

✔ Choose It
The Hawaiian

½ cup lower-sodium marinara sauce (base) + 4 ounces turkey pepperoni slices + 1 cup pineapple chunks (fresh or canned) + ½ cup shredded part-skim mozzarella cheese

212 calories, 1.4g sat fat, 567mg sodium

lose it!
178
CALORIES
SAVED

✔ Choose It
Chicken-Pesto

½ cup prepared pesto (base) + ¾ cup shredded roasted chicken breast + ½ cup sliced red bell pepper + ⅓ cup grated Parmigiano-Reggiano cheese

219 calories, 1.7g sat fat, 364mg sodium

lose it!
171
CALORIES
SAVED

✔ Choose It
BBQ Yardbird

½ cup ready-made barbecue sauce (base) + ½ cup sliced roasted chicken breast + ½ cup shredded cheddar cheese + ½ cup sliced red onion + ½ cup chopped fresh cilantro

205 calories, 1.6g sat fat, 414mg sodium

lose it!
185
CALORIES
SAVED

✔ Choose It
The Farmers' Market

½ cup part-skim ricotta cheese (base) + 2 cups fresh cut asparagus + ½ cup spring peas + 1½ tablespoons olive oil + 2 tablespoons grated lemon rind + ½ cup grated Parmigiano-Reggiano cheese

215 calories, 1.7g sat fat, 334mg sodium

lose it!
175
CALORIES
SAVED

FROZEN ENTRÉES

Frozen entrées and pizzas can be a great solution for a quick, portion-controlled dinner. But read labels carefully: Some meals contain more than one serving. Others may need an extra side dish to be a full, satisfying meal—a good opportunity to bump up your veggie intake and start with a green salad.

lose it!
80
CALORIES SAVED

✘ *Skip It*
Stouffer's® French Bread Pepperoni Pizza
420 calories, 7g sat fat, 810mg sodium

✔ *Choose It*
DiGiorno® Pizzeria!™ Primo Pepperoni Pizza
(1 slice)
340 calories, 6g sat fat, 800mg sodium

✘ Skip It

Newman's Own® General Paul's Chicken Complete Skillet Meal

(1/2 package, 312g)

400 calories, 3g sat fat, 740mg sodium

✘ Skip It

Stouffer's Classic Vegetable Lasagna

400 calories, 7g sat fat, 680mg sodium

✘ Skip It

Marie Callender's® Meat Loaf and Gravy

450 calories, 7g sat fat, 810mg sodium

lose it!
90 CALORIES SAVED

✔ Choose It

Kashi® Steam Meal™ Chicken and Chipotle BBQ

(1/2 package, 284g)

310 calories, 1g sat fat, 620mg sodium

lose it!
150 CALORIES SAVED

✔ Choose It

Amy's® Light & Lean Spinach Lasagna

250 calories, 2.5g sat fat, 540mg sodium

lose it!
210 CALORIES SAVED

✔ Choose It

Lean Cuisine® Meatloaf with Mashed Potatoes

240 calories, 3.5g sat fat, 520mg sodium

BUILD A BETTER PASTA BOWL

Pasta is the solution to many a quick dinner dilemma. Choosing vegetables over meatballs can slim it down and keep it healthy.

✘ Skip It
Traditional Spaghetti & Meatballs

The comfort classic of spaghetti topped with a tomato sauce (enriched with butter and oil), Parmesan, and meatballs sure does pack in the calories and sat fat.

797 calories, 18.4g sat fat, 1,677mg sodium

 SHOP SMART *Choose Whole Grains*

No matter the shape or size, the best pasta choice is a whole-grain variety—one that is labeled "whole wheat" and that lists whole-wheat flour as the first ingredient. Unlike refined pastas, whole-grain noodles don't lose their bran and germ—which carry the healthy fats, protein, antioxidants, B vitamins, minerals, and fiber. Not ready? Start with a whole-grain pasta blend.

 NUTRITION ALERT *Cool Pasta*

Dry pasta's not the only game in town: Many grocery stores carry fresh pasta in the refrigerated sections. They can give a gourmet-feel to your dinner. Be sure to read labels carefully: Stuffed pastas that contain cheese, such as ravioli and tortellini, are generally higher in fat and calories. Look for light varieties that are lower in calories, saturated fat, and sodium.

✔ **Choose It** Pesto Perfect

8 ounces uncooked linguine + 4 ounces fresh baby spinach + 6 tablespoons refrigerated pesto + ¼ cup shredded Parmesan (Serves 4)

352 calories, 3g sat fat, 327mg sodium

lose it!
445
CALORIES
SAVED

✔ **Choose It** Rockin' Ravioli

12 ounces light 4-cheese ravioli + 2 cups steamed broccoli + 2 tablespoons olive oil + 2 tablespoons red wine vinegar + 1 minced garlic clove + 4 sliced plum tomatoes + ¼ cup grated Parmesan cheese (Serves 4)

327 calories, 3.8g sat fat, 467mg sodium

lose it!
470
CALORIES
SAVED

✔ **Choose It** Cheesy Broccoli

8 ounces uncooked penne + ¼ cup grated Parmesan cheese + 2½ ounces shredded cheddar + 1 cup steamed broccoli + ½ teaspoon salt + ¼ teaspoon freshly ground black pepper (Serves 4)

313 calories, 4.9g sat fat, 496mg sodium

lose it!
484
CALORIES
SAVED

LASAGNA

It's the classic comfort food—layers of thick noodles with cheese and meat. But lasagna can also be a great opportunity to add in several servings of vegetables, which ups the vitamins, minerals, antioxidants, and fiber.

✘ Skip It
Classic Lasagna

It's no surprise that lasagna is a heavy, hearty dish. Often made with beef or sausage (or both) and lots of cheese, these rich ingredients can easily add up to an entrée that's high in saturated fat and calories.

603 calories, 17.9g sat fat, 1,135mg sodium

 RIGHT-SIZE-IT *A Smarter Slice*

It's hard to resist serving yourself a large, thick, cheesy piece of lasagna, but that's a big reason why the calorie count on this entrée skyrockets. Stick to smaller portions (about the size of a deck of cards), and go for extra salad or fresh veggies on the side to help fill you up.

✔ Choose It
Turkey Sausage and Spinach Lasagna

Our healthy version is still satisfying for the meat lover. Three cheeses make it indulgent and high in calcium.

ACTIVE 40 MINUTES | TOTAL 1 HOUR, 35 MINUTES

- 1.1 ounces all-purpose flour (about ¼ cup)
- 1 cup 1% low-fat milk
- 1 cup unsalted chicken stock (such as Swanson)
- 1 tablespoon canola oil
- 1 bay leaf
- ¼ teaspoon kosher salt
- ½ teaspoon freshly ground black pepper
- Cooking spray
- 2 tablespoons water
- 1 (12-ounce) package fresh spinach
- 2 (4-ounce) links hot turkey Italian sausage
- ½ cup chopped shallots
- 1 tablespoon minced fresh garlic
- 6 no-boil lasagna noodles
- 1½ cups part-skim ricotta cheese
- 1 ounce shredded part-skim mozzarella cheese
- 1 ounce fresh Parmesan cheese, grated

PREPARATION

1. Preheat oven to 375°.

2. Weigh or lightly spoon flour into a dry measuring cup; level with a knife. Combine flour and next 4 ingredients (through bay leaf) in a medium saucepan over medium heat, stirring with a whisk. Cook 8 minutes or until thick and bubbly, stirring frequently. Remove from heat; stir in salt and pepper. Discard bay leaf. Spread 1 cup milk mixture in bottom of an 11 x 7–inch glass or ceramic baking dish coated with cooking spray.

3. Heat a large skillet over medium heat. Add 2 tablespoons water and spinach to pan; cook 2 minutes or until spinach wilts. Drain spinach, pressing until barely moist. Increase heat to medium-high. Remove casings from sausage. Add sausage to pan; cook 4 minutes or until browned, stirring to crumble. Remove sausage from pan. Add shallots and garlic to pan; sauté 2 minutes. Stir in remaining milk mixture, spinach, and cooked sausage. Remove pan from heat.

4. Arrange 2 noodles over milk mixture in baking dish; top with ½ cup ricotta and one-third spinach mixture. Repeat layers twice. Sprinkle with mozzarella and Parmesan cheeses. Cover with foil coated with cooking spray. Bake at 375° for 40 minutes. Remove foil. Preheat broiler to high. Broil 4 minutes or until cheese is golden brown. Let stand 10 minutes. Serves 6 (serving size: ⅙ of lasagna)

Per serving: 332 calories, 5.9g sat fat, 575mg sodium

TACOS

Tacos are a perennial family favorite: They're easy on the cook and incredibly customizable, so everyone can basically have their own separate meal. The best part? You can stuff them with grilled vegetables, fresh tomatoes, peppers, cabbage, and onions to amp up your veggie servings. Choose a 6-inch corn tortilla, and you'll get a serving of whole grains, too.

✘ Skip It
Classic Taco

A 6-inch corn tortilla stuffed with 2 ounces ground chuck, 2 tablespoons refried beans, and 2 tablespoons cheddar cheese with 1 tablespoon full-fat sour cream and 1 tablespoon guacamole is packed with protein and healthy fat—but here's where too much of a good thing is, well, too much.

323 calories, 8.6g sat fat, 307mg sodium

✔ Choose It
Black Bean Vegetarian

6-inch tortilla + ¼ cup black beans + ¼ cup sautéed sliced zucchini + 2 tablespoons charred corn kernels + 1 tablespoon fresh salsa + 1½ tablespoons feta cheese

134 calories, 2.2g sat fat, 379mg sodium

lose it!
189
CALORIES
SAVED

✔ Choose It
Classic Revisited

6-inch tortilla + 1.5 ounces ground sirloin + 1 tablespoon reduced-fat sour cream + 1 tablespoon Monterey Jack cheese + ½ cup shredded romaine lettuce

185 calories, 4.4g sat fat, 80mg sodium

lose it!
138
CALORIES
SAVED

✔ Choose It
Fajita-Style Steak

6-inch tortilla + 1.5 ounces grilled flank steak + 1 tablespoon guacamole + 1 tablespoon pepper jack cheese + ¼ cup grilled bell peppers and onions

188 calories, 3.1g sat fat, 106mg sodium

lose it!
135
CALORIES
SAVED

✔ Choose It
Shrimp-tastic

6-inch tortilla + 2 ounces grilled shrimp + 2 tablespoons pico de gallo + ¼ cup shredded red cabbage + 1 tablespoon salsa verde + 1 lime wedge

131 calories, 0.3g sat fat, 400mg sodium

lose it!
192
CALORIES
SAVED

BUILD A BETTER RICE BOWL

Rice isn't just a side dish anymore: It makes a great base for a variety of delicious entrées. Use brown rice as the starting point for a good source of whole grains and fiber. No time to cook? No problem: Start with one 8.8-ounce pouch of precooked brown rice, which will serve four, and try some of these toppings.

✗ *Skip It* Beef and Black Beans

Topping your rice with ground beef, shredded cheddar cheese, black beans, and jarred salsa can lead to more calories and sodium than you might expect.

Per serving: 456 calories, 11.6g sat fat, 1,118mg sodium

✔ *Choose It* Tex-Mex

8 ounces ground sirloin (cooked and seasoned with 1¼ tablespoons 40% less-sodium taco seasoning) + ¼ cup charred corn kernels + 15-ounce can organic black beans, rinsed and drained + 1 cup fresh pico de gallo + 1 minced jalapeño pepper + 2 tablespoons chopped fresh cilantro (Serves 4)

Per serving: 363 calories, 3.7g sat fat, 502mg sodium

✔ *Choose It* Chicken and Broccoli

1 pound skinless, boneless chicken breast (cut into bite-sized pieces, seasoned with ¼ teaspoon kosher salt and ¼ teaspoon black pepper, and cooked in 1 tablespoon olive oil) + 3 cups broccoli florets, steamed + ½ cup chopped green onions + 4 ounces melted light processed cheese (such as Velveeta Light) + 2 tablespoons toasted sliced almonds (Serves 4)

Per serving: 355 calories, 3g sat fat, 668mg sodium

POTATOES

Potatoes have been demonized as the white starch to avoid at all costs, but remember, they are a vegetable, after all, and filled with nutrients. Baby potatoes are a great base for a delicious side dish, but popular mix-ins like bacon and cheese can pack on the calories and sat fat.

✗ Skip It
Buttery Bacon Potatoes

Bacon and potatoes are a delicious pairing, but the traditional recipe adds up to a starchy calorie and fat bomb.

365 calories, 13.7g sat fat, 371mg sodium

 NUTRITION ALERT *Eat the Skin*

That's where the bulk of the nutrients are. Of course with baby potatoes, you automatically eat the skin, but remember to eat the skin of regular potatoes, too. The flesh of a medium-sized baked potato contains about 17% of the potassium, a third of the vitamin C, and almost 11% of the niacin you need for the day.

 SHOP SMART *A Better French Fry*

Yes, it is possible for French fries to be healthier: Take a look in the frozen foods section, and you'll find a variety of better-for-you versions. That's partly because when they're frozen, you're placing them on a baking sheet to bake them instead of frying in oil. Choose brands like Ore-Ida, Alexia, and Whole Foods' 365 that have 130 to 140 calories and 5g fat per serving. You can also choose sweet potato fries.

lose it!
315
CALORIES
SAVED

✔ *Choose It*
Baby Potatoes with Arugula Pesto

Our homemade arugula pesto gives potatoes great color and flavor without the fat.

ACTIVE 30 MINUTES | TOTAL 1 HOUR

- 1 pound baby potatoes, halved
- 1 cup arugula
- ½ cup fresh basil
- 2 tablespoons grated fresh Parmesan
- 2 tablespoons unsalted chicken stock
- 1 tablespoon olive oil
- 1 tablespoon fresh lemon juice
- ⅜ teaspoon salt
- ¼ teaspoon freshly ground black pepper

PREPARATION

Place potatoes in a saucepan; cover with water. Bring to a boil. Cook 11 minutes; drain. Pulse arugula, basil, Parmesan, chicken stock, olive oil, lemon juice, salt, and pepper in a mini food processor. Combine potatoes and arugula mixture in a medium bowl; toss. Serves 4 (serving size: ¾ cup)

Per serving: 50 calories, 2g sat fat, 299mg sodium

MASHED POTATOES

Mashed potatoes are a classic comfort food, and just because you're trying to eat healthier doesn't mean you have to miss out. Use this easy base recipe to get started: Place 4 (6-ounce) baking potatoes, peeled and cut into 1-inch pieces, in a large microwave-safe bowl. Cover bowl with plastic wrap; cut a 1-inch slit in center of plastic wrap. Microwave at HIGH 10 minutes. Let stand for 2 minutes. Mash with a potato masher. You'll get four 1-cup servings that serve as a wonderful base for all sorts of mix-ins.

✗ Skip It
Classic Mashed Potatoes

With milk, butter, sour cream, *and* cheddar, traditional mashed spuds are rich and creamy, but you're paying a high price in calories and sat fat.

333 calories, 12.9g sat fat, 791mg sodium

🛒 SHOP SMART
Packaged Potatoes

Mashed, sliced, diced, or fried—refrigerated and frozen potatoes come in many forms. The healthiest options have potatoes listed first in the ingredients list and use vegetable or canola oil—not partially hydrogenated oil. The nutrition stats on these potato products should look something like this: less than 1g saturated fat and no more than 300mg of sodium per serving.

✔ *Choose It*
Bacon & Reduced-Fat Cheddar

¹/₄ cup shredded reduced-fat extra-sharp cheddar cheese + 1 slice center-cut bacon, cooked and crumbled + ¹/₂ cup reduced-fat sour cream + ¹/₂ cup 1% low-fat milk + 2 tablespoons fresh chopped chives + ¹/₂ teaspoon black pepper + ¹/₂ teaspoon salt (Serves 4)

Per serving: 254 calories, 3.7g sat fat, 280mg sodium

lose it!
79
CALORIES SAVED

✔ *Choose It*
Edamame

1¹/₂ cups cooked shelled edamame pureed with ¹/₄ cup fat-free, lower-sodium chicken broth + ¹/₃ cup 2% reduced-fat milk + 1 tablespoon olive oil + ¹/₄ teaspoon salt + ¹/₈ teaspoon white pepper (Serves 4)

Per serving: 238 calories, 0.8g sat fat, 220mg sodium

lose it!
95
CALORIES SAVED

✔ *Choose It*
Roasted Garlic

³/₄ cup 1% low-fat milk + ¹/₄ cup coarsely chopped roasted garlic cloves (find them in the salad bar in many grocery stores) + 1 tablespoon chopped fresh sage + ¹/₂ teaspoon salt + ¹/₂ teaspoon black pepper (Serves 4)

Per serving: 223 calories, 0.7g sat fat, 329mg sodium

lose it!
110
CALORIES SAVED

✔ *Choose It*
Southwest

2 tablespoons 1% low-fat milk + ³/₄ cup plain low-fat yogurt + 1 tablespoon chopped canned chipotle chile in adobo sauce + ¹/₂ teaspoon black pepper + ¹/₄ teaspoon salt + ¹/₄ teaspoon ground cumin (Serves 4)

Per serving: 206 calories, 0.6g sat fat, 236mg sodium

lose it!
127
CALORIES SAVED

GREEN BEANS

Green beans are a vegetable even some of the pickiest eaters like. But efforts to jazz up the basic green bean can add hefty calories and fat. One cup of green beans is just 31 calories, so you have lots of room to add flavorful, healthy toppings to make a tasty and satisfying side dish.

✖ Skip It

Green Bean Casserole

The simple green bean often gets piled with cheese, butter, and sour cream, taking this nutritious bean to another realm.

**416 calories,
19.1g sat fat,
901mg sodium**

SHOP SMART

Packaged Vegetables

It's always best to go fresh when it comes to fruits and vegetables, but frozen can be a good option if you buy in bulk and need to have vegetables at the ready for longer periods of time. Try to avoid canned vegetables if possible: They tend to be high in sodium and lose their texture.

lose it!
312
CALORIES
SAVED

✔ *Choose It*

Ginger-Sesame Green Bean Stir-Fry

A few high-flavored ingredients enliven this quick side dish without adding fat.

ACTIVE 15 MINUTES | TOTAL 15 MINUTES

- 1 tablespoon sesame oil
- 1 pound green beans, trimmed
- 1 tablespoon toasted sesame seeds
- 1 tablespoon minced peeled fresh ginger
- 1 tablespoon tahini
- 5 teaspoons lower-sodium soy sauce
- 1 tablespoon water
- 1 tablespoon fresh lime juice

PREPARATION

Heat a skillet over medium-high heat. Add sesame oil; swirl to coat pan. Add green beans; cook 7 minutes or until beans begin to brown. Combine sesame seeds, ginger, tahini, soy sauce, water, and lime juice in a bowl. Add mixture to pan. Cook 1 minute; toss to coat. Serves 4 (serving size: about 1 cup)

Per serving: 104 calories, 1g sat fat, 231mg sodium

CHINESE

With so many dishes that have vegetables as their base, how can you go wrong at a Chinese restaurant? It's often the sauce that drives the calorie, saturated fat, and sodium counts way up. Going with sauce on the side is a safer bet. Ordering wisely and limiting your portion size help, too.

✗ *Skip It*

Sweet and Sour Chicken

Take one look at this dish, and you know it's not healthy. Chicken is a lean protein, but in this entrée it's battered, deep fried, and smothered in a gooey, sugary sauce. After a meal this heavy, a nap may be in order.

1,032 calories

✔ Choose It
Sweet and Sour Chicken

Powdered peanut butter adds richness here, but you can substitute more flour.

ACTIVE 23 MINUTES | TOTAL 23 MINUTES

- ¼ cup mirin (sweet rice wine) or ¼ cup dry sherry mixed with 2 teaspoons sugar
- 1 large egg, lightly beaten
- 1 pound skinless, boneless chicken breast tenders, cut into 2-inch pieces
- ¼ cup powdered peanut butter
- 3 tablespoons quick-mixing flour (such as Wondra)
- 3 tablespoons cornstarch
- 1 tablespoon sugar
- 3 tablespoons canola oil
- ¾ cup sliced green onions
- 1 red bell pepper, chopped
- 5 tablespoons water
- 3 tablespoons ketchup
- 2 tablespoons Sriracha
- 1 tablespoon plum sauce
- 1 teaspoon Worcestershire sauce
- 1 (8.8-ounce) package precooked white rice
- ¼ cup cilantro leaves
- 2 tablespoons toasted sesame seeds

lose it!
558
**CALORIES
SAVED**

PREPARATION

1. Combine mirin and egg in a medium bowl, stirring with a whisk. Add chicken; toss to coat. Let stand 5 minutes; drain well.

2. Combine powdered peanut butter and next 3 ingredients (through sugar) in a bowl, stirring with a whisk. Add chicken; toss well to coat. Heat a large skillet over medium-high heat. Add oil to pan; swirl to coat. Add chicken; cook 3 minutes on each side or until done. Remove chicken from pan; keep warm.

3. Heat pan over high heat. Add onions and bell pepper; stir-fry 1 minute. Combine water and next 4 ingredients (through Worcestershire) in a bowl, stirring with a whisk. Add chicken and ketchup mixture to pan; cook 1 minute, tossing to coat.

4. Divide rice evenly among 4 plates; top evenly with chicken mixture. Sprinkle evenly with cilantro leaves and sesame seeds. Serves 4 (serving size: 1 cup chicken and ½ cup rice)

Per serving: 474 calories

ITALIAN

A heaping plate of pasta is what eating out Italian is all about. But, that mound of pasta along with a rich sauce and toppings can cost more than you think. Classic Fettuccine Alfredo can weigh in at 1,220 calories, but swap in marinara for the cream sauce and the fat and calories plummet. Other simple changes: Ask for less cheese, and half your portion.

lose it!
369
CALORIES SAVED

✖ *Skip It*
Spaghetti Carbonara

This pasta dish is silky with egg and melted cheese with a salty, rich kick from pancetta or bacon. But, it's also a splurge that doesn't leave much room for starters, sides, salads, or the ubiquitous bread basket with olive oil and herbs for dipping.

820 calories

✔ *Choose It*
Linguine Aglio e Olio

"Garlic and oil" seems basic, however the flavor is anything but: Olive oil, garlic, and hot pepper add zest and healthful fats to this simple and satisfying dish. Pair it with a side of steamed spinach or broccoli to add fiber, bulk, and nutrients like vitamin C, potassium, and magnesium—even a bit of extra calcium—to your meal.

451 calories

MEXICAN

Here's the trick to keeping your healthy-eating intentions from taking a siesta at the cantina: Many of the ingredients highest in sodium are also high in calories and saturated fat, which means that cutting back on cheese, sour cream, and chips solves three problems at once. Plus, most dishes are easily customized.

lose it!
590
CALORIES SAVED

✘ *Skip It*
Cheese and Bean Enchilada

Don't let this vegetarian option fool you: Tons of cheese can add just as much saturated fat as meat— not to mention sodium and calories. A typical serving gives you over a day's worth of saturated fat and nearly 1,600mg of sodium.

910 calories

✔ *Choose It*
Beef Taco

Surprise! Beef can be best. Taco shells are smaller and lower in calories than a flour or corn tortilla, and beef tacos usually have fewer calories than the fish variety (which are often fried). So you have more room for rice and beans and a (small) margarita.

320 calories

BURGER KING®

You can get more for your money if you order a meal, but you also get more fat and calories, too. In general, it's best to order items separately, and keep an eye on your sides. The healthiest side is apple slices (30 calories, 0g sat fat), but a value-sized portion of onion rings (150 calories, 1.5g sat fat) is also a better option than small French fries (290 calories, 2.5g sat fat).

lose it!
875
CALORIES SAVED

✘ Skip It
Double Whopper® Sandwich meal

Sure, you get two whopper patties, French fries, and a soda, but that's almost the amount of calories and fat you should be eating in an entire day! And that's the *small* Whopper meal.

1,500 calories, 22g sat fat, 1,550mg sodium

✔ Choose It
Whopper® Junior meal with light lemonade and small onion rings

Not a super-healthy choice, but certainly the lesser of the evils when you're craving a hamburger and fries. Small-sizing your meal and going with a light drink and onion rings trims major calories and fat.

625 calories, 7.5g sat fat, 1,300mg sodium

CHILI'S®

You can get your Mexican food fix here, along with flavorful twists on chicken, beef, and seafood staples. Chili's also offers Lighter Choice, which includes options for less than 650 calories. But remember that's just for the entrée—for most people, that's enough calories for a whole meal.

lose it!
1,270
CALORIES SAVED

✗ *Skip It*
Bacon Ranch Beef Quesadilla

Flour tortillas stuffed with marinated steak, three cheeses, smoked bacon, and Ranch dressing result in a huge calorie and sodium load.

1,880 calories, 47g sat fat, 3,990mg sodium

✔ *Choose It*
Margarita Grilled Chicken

The margarita grilled chicken with pico de gallo, tortilla strips, rice, and black beans brings the calorie count way down, but it is still pretty high in sodium so watch your intake the rest of the day.

610 Calories, 3g sat fat, 2,450mg sodium

MCDONALD'S®

Hard to believe, but the Big Mac® isn't the worst offender when it comes to the hamburgers at McDonald's. However, there are more reasonable options to pick from. Just be mindful of what's on the sandwich: extra cheese and creamy sauces add unnecessary calories and fat.

lose it!
200
CALORIES
SAVED

✘ *Skip It*
Double Quarter Pounder® with Cheese

Two beef patties, two slices of cheese with pickles, onions, and ketchup sound simple enough. But thanks to the sheer amount of meat bulging between the two buns, this burger has even more calories than the famous Big Mac, which runs 550 calories—and that's including the special sauce!

740 calories, 19g sat fat, 1,300mg sodium

✔ *Choose It*
Deluxe Quarter Pounder

You still get the meatiness of the quarter pounder, but also the creaminess of mayo and real slices of red onion and tomato, which earn you slightly more nutrients and fiber.

540 calories, 11g sat fat, 940mg sodium

ORDER SMART AT MCDONALD'S

• UNDER 350-CALORIE BURGER McDonald's has gone beyond Big Macs and Quarter Pounders. The restaurant now offers the Grilled Onion Cheddar Burger, which has some unique toppings, and at 300 calories, is one of the lowest-calorie burger options on the menu. It also has 6g sat fat and 640mg sodium. The McDonald's Hamburger (240 calories, 3g sat fat, 480mg sodium) is by far one of the better options here. The Cheeseburger also has 290 calories, but the cheese brings the sodium up to 680mg.

• DOUBLE HAPPINESS Try these other sandwiches that feature two beef patties on a bun:
Double Cheeseburger: 430 calories, 10g sat fat, 1,040mg sodium
Daily Double: 430 calories, 9g sat fat, 760mg sodium (includes mayonnaise and a thick slice of tomato)
McDouble®: 380 calories, 8g sat fat, 840mg sodium

• WHAT ABOUT THE HAPPY MEAL? As with the adult-sized combo meals, it is better to leave off the sides and soda. McDonald's has come under fire for Happy Meals that are high in calories, fat, and sodium so they've increased the availability of fruit or yogurt as side options.

• SALAD VS BURGER Salads make up a very small percentage of the sales at McDonald's, but they can be a good choice as long as you steer clear of the Premium Southwest Salad with Crispy Chicken and Newman's Own® Ranch Dressing which at 620 calories packs in more than the burgers mentioned above. Instead, choose a Southwest Salad with Grilled Chicken with low-fat Balsamic Vinaigrette for a more moderate 325-calorie meal.

 NUTRITION ALERT

That Has How Many Calories?!
Another burger that comes in with a higher calorie count than the Big Mac: The Bacon Habanero Ranch Quarter Pounder—610 calories, 13g sat fat, 1,190mg sodium. The bakery-style bun alone adds 200 calories, and the bacon adds 100 calories.

OLIVE GARDEN^{SM}

Sampling from the smorgasboard of appetizers is what Olive Garden is all about, but be sure to share: Some of these have the calorie, fat, and sodium count of a main dish!

lose it!
160
CALORIES SAVED

✗ *Skip It*
Grilled Chicken Flatbread
760 calories, 15g sat fat, 1,500mg sodium

✓ *Choose It*
Caprese Flatbread
600 calories, 10g sat fat, 1,430mg sodium

 ORDER SMART *Dipping Sauces*

You can't eat Olive Garden's famous delicious and garlicky breadsticks without dipping sauce, but be mindful about the calories: Marinara's the healthiest by far at 80 calories, 0g sat fat, 480mg sodium. Next up is the Five Cheese Marinara at 190 calories, 8g sat fat, 520mg sodium. Dip very sparingly in the Alfredo, which runs 460 calories, 27g sat fat, 590mg sodium.

 NUTRITION ALERT *Appetizer Overload*

Even though appetizers are for sharing, these Olive Garden apps are so eye-poppingly high in calories, fat, and sodium that you'd better have a big party of people to share with:
• Lasagna Fritta: 1,030 calories, 21g sat fat, 1,590mg sodium
• Smoked Mozzarella Fonduta: 940 calories, 28g sat fat, 1,940mg sodium
• Calamari: 890 calories, 5g sat fat, 2,340mg sodium

✗ *Skip It*
Spicy Shrimp Scampi Fritta
560 calories, 6g sat fat, 1,920mg sodium

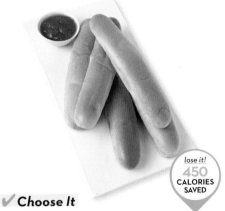

✗ *Skip It*
Bruschetta
680 calories, 6g sat fat, 2,480mg sodium

lose it!
190
CALORIES
SAVED

✓ *Choose It*
Fried Zucchini
370 calories, 2g sat fat, 620mg sodium

lose it!
450
CALORIES
SAVED

✓ *Choose It*
Breadstick with Garlic-Butter
spread *(and side of marinara sauce)*
230 calories, 0.5g sat fat, 930mg sodium

OLIVE GARDEN^{SM}

Italian-style dinners can absolutely be healthy and chock-full of monounsaturated and polyunsaturated fats found in olives and olive oil as well as antioxidants from garlic and tomato sauce. But be careful of big portions and loads of cheese.

lose it!
540
CALORIES SAVED

✘ Skip It
Steak Gorgonzola Alfredo
1,380 calories, 50g sat fat, 2,810mg sodium

✔ Choose It
Steak Toscano
840 calories, 20g sat fat, 1,360mg sodium

ORDER SMART *A Lighter Lasagna*

Typical meat lasagna usually packs in the calories and fat, and the Lasagna Classico at Olive Garden is no exception: The dinner portion runs 960 calories, 31g sat fat, and 2,360mg sodium. Thankfully, they offer a Lasagna Primavera with Grilled Chicken, which is a much more digestible 560 calories, 10g sat fat, and 1,700mg sodium.

lose it!
410
CALORIES
SAVED

✗ *Skip It*
Five-Cheese Ziti al Forno
1,150 calories, 35g sat fat, 1,930mg sodium

✔ *Choose It*
Cheese Ravioli with Marinara Sauce
740 calories, 13g sat fat, 1,380mg sodium

 ORDER SMART *Seafood Stars*

Eating fish is a great way to get a dose of heart-healthy omega-3 fatty acids, and luckily Olive Garden has a few lower-calorie seafood options including Herb-Grilled Salmon (540 calories, 6g sat fat, 500mg sodium) and Baked Tilapia with Shrimp (360 calories, 6g sat fat, 980mg sodium).

OUTBACK STEAKHOUSE®

It's surprisingly easy to choose lower-calorie meals at a steakhouse. Size is key: Keep your steak small (6 ounces or less), and you can have a reasonably healthy steak dinner with room for a starter salad and sides to boot!

lose it!
302
CALORIES SAVED

✘ Skip It

12-ounce Sirloin and Grilled Shrimp

The cut of this meat isn't bad—it's the size that makes it a not-so-great option. The high calorie count is not helped by the addition of a side of fries (380 calories, 8.5g sat fat, 531mg sodium).

874 calories, 16.3g sat fat, 1,286mg sodium

✔ Choose It

Filet and Grilled Shrimp on the Barbie

Combining the 6-oz. steak with shrimp gives you lots of protein plus a dose of healthy fats. Grilling also keeps the calories and fat count low. (A side of steamed broccoli adds 118 calories.)

572 calories, 10.3g sat fat, 981mg sodium

ORDER SMART AT OUTBACK STEAKHOUSE

• **BETTER DINNER CHOICES** Obviously Outback has many steak options, but skip the 16-ounce Herb Roasted Prime Rib au Jus and its 1,403 calories, 52g sat fat, and 1,514mg sodium for the far better 6-ounce steaks. Go for the Outback Special, a 6-ounce sirloin, with 254 calories, 4.9g sat fat, 226mg sodium or the Victoria's Filet® with 218 calories, 3.9g sat fat, and 206mg sodium. Add the tasty Wild Mushroom Sauce for just 42 calories more.

• **GO SEAFOOD** Some of the healthiest diets in the world have one thing in common: seafood. While fish is low in calories and saturated fat, it all depends on the preparation. Some of the fish entrées at Outback are surprisingly high in sodium. Keep it simple and stick with grilled. The Perfectly Grilled Salmon is your best choice here with 387 calories, 4g sat fat, and 295mg sodium.

• **APPETIZERS TO AVOID** The entrées aren't the danger zone at Outback, it's the appetizers! All the starters are pretty high in calories and fat. Even though they're meant to share, you'd have to measure out each person's portion pretty carefully to make sure you don't end up eating an entrée's worth of calories.
A few red flags:

Regular-sized Aussie Cheese Fries: At 1,913 calories, 58g sat fat, and 2,775mg sodium, you're better off steering clear—unless you can eat just a few.

Bloomin' Onion®: Yes, this is what they're famous for, but if you're going to splurge, you should eat lightly for the rest of the day. The whole fried onion is 1,948 calories, 48g sat fat, and 4,085mg sodium! Even divided by four, that's 326 calories per person.

Spinach and Artichoke Dip: With dips, it's really hard to keep track of how much you're eating, and this favorite is 888 calories, 20g sat fat, and 1,923mg sodium—and that's before you dip anything into it!

P.F. CHANG'S®

The dishes at P.F. Chang's are meant to be shared, but choosing the lower-calorie options means you'll eat less overall. Don't forget to factor in rice: A 6-ounce serving of brown or white adds 300 calories. Go with brown for more whole grains and eat half the bowl.

lose it!
130
CALORIES SAVED

✗ Skip It
Pan-Fried Pork Dumplings with Sauce
420 calories, 5g sat fat, 1,200mg sodium

✔ Choose It
Steamed Shrimp Dumplings
290 calories, 0.5g sat fat, 1,030mg sodium

🥡 ORDER SMART *Sauce Savvy*

Sodium is always a concern at restaurants, and Chinese cuisine is no exception. Here, sauces run up the sodium numbers: At 1,000mg per tablespoon, soy sauce packs a hefty sodium punch. Lower-sodium soy sauce is a bit better at 500mg per tablespoon, but stick with a small packet of Chinese mustard, duck sauce, or chili sauce, which boost flavor without as much sodium.

🍎 NUTRITION ALERT
That Has How Many Calories?!

Vegetarian dishes are usually low-cal options at restaurants, but one glance P.F. Chang's offerings proves otherwise—unless you order your meal steamed. The Coconut Curry Vegetables clock in at 1,050 calories, 24g sat fat, and 1,360mg sodium. The only vegetarian dish that lives up to its healthy halo is the stir-fried Buddha's Feast, with 420 calories and 12g sat fat, but it's really salty at 3,440mg sodium.

✗ *Skip It*

2 Egg Rolls with sauce

350 calories, 2g sat fat, 1,305mg sodium

✗ *Skip It*

Kung Pao Chicken

1,070 calories, 10g sat fat, 2,410mg sodium

✗ *Skip It*

Walnut Shrimp with Melon

1,380 calories, 16g sat fat, 1,830mg sodium

lose it!
40
CALORIES
SAVED

✔ *Choose It*

2 Spring Rolls with sauce

Skip the sauce to bring down sodium.

310 calories, 1g sat fat, 1,530mg sodium

lose it!
180
CALORIES
SAVED

✔ *Choose It*

Sesame Chicken

890 calories, 6g sat fat, 2,250mg sodium

lose it!
620
CALORIES
SAVED

✔ *Choose It*

Crispy Honey Shrimp

760 calories, 4g sat fat, 1,320mg sodium

PIZZA HUT®

Pizza can easily be an indulgence, but for the most part, it's easy to put together a healthy pie. At Pizza Hut, it's all about the thickness of the crust and the toppings. Go easy on the cheese, thin on the crust, and choose toppings wisely, and you've got a tasty, nutrient-packed meal.

lose it!
60
CALORIES SAVED

✘ *Skip It*
Meat Lover's® 14-inch Large Pan Pizza *(1 slice)*

Three meats and a super-thick crust with tons of cheese make this slice the highest in calories, fat, and sodium.

470 calories, 10g sat fat, 1,150mg sodium

✔ *Choose It*
Supreme *(1 slice)*

The Supreme still gives you loads of meat and cheese, but is a slightly better choice.

410 calories, 8g sat fat, 910mg sodium

lose it!
140
CALORIES SAVED

✗ *Skip It*
Supreme 6-inch Personal Pan Pizza
730 calories, 14g sat fat, 1,710mg sodium

✔ *Choose It*
Chicken Supreme Personal Pan Pizza
590 calories, 8g sat fat, 1,370mg sodium

NUTRITION ALERT *Crusts*

Between the Cheddar Crust, 3-Cheese Stuffed Crust, Hand-Tossed, and Regular Crust, Pizza Hut offers a mind-blowing number of options. But no matter what the topping, the best choice remains the thin crust. You save 50 calories and 200mg of sodium by opting for the thin over regular crust—without sacrificing flavor.

RED LOBSTER®

It's all seafood, so it's all healthy, right? Well, no. Obviously anything fried is going to be super-high in calories and fat, but various cuts of seafood are more caloric and salty than others, too. Going for a surf-and-turf combo also takes down the diet-friendly quotient of your meal.

lose it!
470
CALORIES SAVED

✘ *Skip It*
NY Strip and Rock Lobster Tail
890 calories, 15g sat fat, 2,200mg sodium

✔ *Choose It*
Peppercorn-Grilled Sirloin with 2 Maine Lobster Tails
420 calories, 5g sat fat, 1,450mg sodium

 ORDER SMART *Dipping Sauces*

When it comes to seafood, choose your dipping sauce wisely. Here's how 1½ ounces of Red Lobster's options stack up:
- 100% pure melted butter (unsalted): 300 calories, 21g sat fat, 280mg sodium
- Mayonnaise: 300 calories, 4.5g sat fat, 220mg sodium
- Tartar sauce: 210 calories, 3g sat fat, 180mg sodium

 NUTRITION ALERT *Potato Sides*

Red Lobster's three potato side dishes—mashed potatoes, crispy red potatoes, and a baked potato—all have about 200 calories. The difference is in the sodium: The plain baked potato actually comes in the lowest at 310mg, then the mashed potatoes at 620mg, and the crispy red potatoes clock in at 1,020mg.

✗ *Skip It*

New England Clam Chowder *(bowl)*

400 calories, 16g sat fat, 1,500mg sodium

✗ *Skip It*

Hand-Battered Fish and Chips

700 calories, 3g sat fat, 1,030mg sodium

lose it!
240
CALORIES
SAVED

✔ *Choose It*

Manhattan Clam Chowder *(bowl)*

160 calories, 1g sat fat, 1,420mg sodium

lose it!
340
CALORIES
SAVED

✔ *Choose It*

Parmesan-Crusted Tilapia

360 calories, 5g sat fat, 900mg sodium

TGI FRIDAYS℠

Fridays has a huge menu with lots of variety—which means lots of healthy and unhealthy dishes. But there are surprises here: Dishes that might sound healthy turned out not to be. (Check out the Crispy Green Bean Fries.) It all depends on how the dish is prepared.

lose it!
860
CALORIES SAVED

✘ Skip It
Hibachi Chicken Skewers
1,230 calories, 4g sat fat, 3,900mg sodium

✔ Choose It
6-ounce Sirloin
370 calories, 12g sat fat, 860mg sodium

ORDER SMART *The Sides Story*

Surprisingly, the fries at Fridays aren't too high in calories (with the exception of the Parmesan Steak Fries, which run 660 calories, 10g sat fat, and 630mg sodium). Share, and you'll eat even less. In fact, they're lower in calories than a rice pilaf. Here's the countdown for the lower-calorie choices:
- Sweet Potato Fries: 390 calories, 9g sat fat, 230mg sodium
- Seasoned Fries: 290 calories, 4.5g sat fat, 980mg sodium

NUTRITION ALERT

That Has How Much Salt?!

You'll notice that even though you're saving calories and fat on most of these dishes, the sodium numbers are still extremely high. The Jack Daniel's* premium entrées and grill dishes are particularly so: The Jack Daniel's Ribeye and Crispy Shrimp comes in at 2,140mg sodium—not to mention 890 calories and 8.5g sat fat, and the Jack Daniel's Ribs and Shrimp has 4,140mg sodium!

✗ Skip It
Crispy Green Bean Fries
(individual appetizer)
900 calories, 21g sat fat, 1,720mg sodium

✗ Skip It
Pecan-Crusted Chicken Salad
1,080 calories, 16g sat fat, 1,650mg sodium

lose it!
520
CALORIES SAVED

✔ Choose It
Spinach Florentine Flatbread
380 calories, 11g sat fat, 800mg sodium

lose it!
580
CALORIES SAVED

✔ Choose It
Balsamic-Glazed Chicken Caesar
500 calories, 7g sat fat, 1,340mg sodium

WENDY'S®

*The great thing about Wendy's is that their hamburgers come in many sizes.
Plus, you can customize your meal from the ground up. Start with a hamburger patty,
add ketchup and mustard (skip the mayo), and pile on the tomato, lettuce,
onion, and pickles for a bit of nutrition and flavor.*

lose it!
550
**CALORIES
SAVED**

✘ *Skip It*
Baconator®

Any hamburger topped with bacon can't be healthy,
plus with the Baconator you have two patties plus
mayonnaise plus cheese. It all adds up fast and even
contains 2.5g of trans fat—the worst kind.

940 calories, 23g sat fat, 1,850mg sodium

✔ *Choose It*
Junior Bacon Cheeseburger

With a smaller beef patty, the calories, fat, and sodium
get dialed down even though you still have bacon and
cheese.

390 calories, 8g sat fat, 850mg sodium

ORDER SMART AT WENDY'S

• **WATCH THE BUN...AND THE BACON** Wendy's has been experimenting with different breads for their burgers, and the most popular of their new offerings just might be the Pretzel Bacon Cheeseburger with its soft-pretzel bun. While not the worst offender on their menu, the Pretzel Bacon Cheeseburger has 680 calories, 15g of sat fat, and 1,100mg sodium. The Baconator is even worse at 940 calories, 23g sat fat, and 1,850mg sodium, and its offspring, the Son of Baconator®, not much better at 660 calories, 15g sat fat, and 1,640mg sodium.

• **THE JUNIOR CHOICE** When in doubt, go junior. All of Wendy's junior burgers (except the Junior Bacon Cheeseburger) are 350 calories or less. Trim even more calories by skipping half or all of the bun.

• **THAT HAS HOW MANY CALORIES?** Dave's Hot 'n' Juicy™ ¾-pound triple comes in at 1,090 calories, 29g sat fat, and 1,990mg sodium. The issue here is the amount of meat: 3 beef patties plus cheese and mayonnaise make this hamburger eat up almost your entire day's worth of calories and go over the amount of salt and fat you should have in 24 hours.

• **SKIP THE CHEESE AND CREAMY DRESSINGS** Wendy's has a number of great salad choices, but also some that are loaded with fat and sodium. Luckily, they do let you customize them. Stick with lighter dressings, skip the cheese, and order a half size to bring these back to earth. Your best bet is the Apple Pecan Chicken Salad (without cheese).

 NUTRITION ALERT *Baked Potato vs. French Fries*

Take advantage of the various spuds on the menu and sub in a Sour Cream and Chive Baked Potato (320 calories, 2g sat fat, 50mg sodium) for French fries. The potato is just as hearty as a medium French fry (410 calories, 3.5g sat fat, 440mg sodium), but you get more filling fiber and protein with the potato.

A WELL-CHOSEN SNACK CAN BE THE BEST THING TO KEEP YOU SATISFIED. FROZEN YOGURT WITH FRUIT IS LIGHT AND GOOD FOR YOU.

SNACKS & SWEETS

"Everything in moderation" couldn't be truer when it comes to treats, whether they are sweet, salty, or savory. Making room in your everyday diet for snacks and desserts is important so you never feel deprived. The key, however, is learning to satisfy your cravings without going overboard on calories or fat. Indulge wisely, and you can have your cake (or chips or ice cream) and eat them, too.

EVERYDAY SNACKS

Keeping your kitchen stocked with healthy foods—packaged and fresh—is key to snacking right. Portion control is also crucial, particularly because so many snackable foods (chips, crackers, trail mix) come in big bags with multiple servings.

lose it!
104
CALORIES SAVED

✘ Skip It
Chocolate Almonds
(2 handfuls)
244 calories, 7g sat fat, 12mg sodium

✔ Choose It
Graham Cracker, Hazelnut, Nuts
(1 graham cracker sheet with 2 teaspoons chocolate-hazelnut spread and 1 teaspoon chopped nuts)
140 calories, 1.6g sat fat, 72mg sodium

 RIGHT-SIZE-IT *Perfect Portions*

Try to choose snacks that come in single-serve containers, since that's built-in portion control. If only big bags are available, remember that one serving fits comfortably into the palm of your hand. To keep a lid on portions, go for snacks that take a while to eat, like pistachios (it takes time to shell them) and vegetable strips in dip (you have to pause to dip each strip).

✗ *Skip It*

Dried Apricots or Pears
(½ cup)
157 calories, 0g sat fat, 7mg sodium

✗ *Skip It*

Chips & Guacamole
(1 ounce chips with 3 tablespoons guacamole)
215 calories, 4.8g sat fat, 480mg sodium

✗ *Skip It*

Dry-Roasted Salted Peanuts
(¼ cup)
213 calories, 1.3g sat fat, 153mg sodium

lose it!
107
CALORIES SAVED

✔ *Choose It*

Fresh Fruit
(3 apricots or 1 pear)
50 calories, 0g sat fat, 1mg sodium

lose it!
115
CALORIES SAVED

✔ *Choose It*

Toast & Avocado
(1 whole-grain slice with 2 avocado slices)
100 calories, 0.6g sat fat, 135mg sodium

lose it!
148
CALORIES SAVED

✔ *Choose It*

Edamame
(½ cup shelled edamame sprinkled with 1 teaspoon toasted sesame seeds)
65 calories, 0g sat fat, 4mg sodium

EVERYDAY SNACKS

Mixing packaged and fresh foods makes for multiple snack options. Making your own versions is one key to saving calories and fat—even boosting taste and texture.

lose it!
90
CALORIES SAVED

✘ *Skip It*
Chocolate Ice Cream
(½ cup full-fat ice cream)
150 calories, 4.5g sat fat, 45mg sodium

✔ *Choose It*
Fudge Pop
60 calories, 1g sat fat, 55mg sodium

 SHOP SMART *Ingredient Labels*

Generally, the least-processed packaged foods, which are the healthier options, have the fewest ingredients. So when you're browsing the snack aisle, check labels carefully and choose products with a short list of ingredients. And make sure you recognize most of the items on the list!

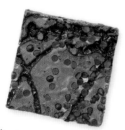

✘ *Skip It*
Brownie

270 calories, 4g sat fat, 200mg sodium

✘ *Skip It*
Cheese Crackers
(1 pack)

200 calories, 3.5g sat fat, 330mg sodium

✘ *Skip It*
Traditional Trail Mix
(¹/₂ cup with nuts, dried fruit, and chocolate)

353 calories, 4.5g sat fat, 88mg sodium

lose it!
91 CALORIES SAVED

✔ *Choose It*
Creme-Filled Cookies & Milk

(2 chocolate creme cookies and 8 ounces fat-free milk)

179 calories, 1g sat fat, 223mg sodium

lose it!
94 CALORIES SAVED

✔ *Choose It*
Flatbread Crackers, Ricotta, Honey

(2 multigrain crackers with 2 tablespoons part-skim ricotta and 1 teaspoon honey)

106 calories, 1.5g sat fat, 92mg sodium

lose it!
143 CALORIES SAVED

✔ *Choose It*
Trail Mix & Whole-Grain Cereal

(blend half traditional trail mix with ¹/₃ cup whole-grain cereal)

210 calories, 2.3g sat fat, 124mg sodium

SNACK MIXES

Snack mixes are a fun, flavorful treat for everyone. From crunchy crackers to sweet chocolate chips, ingredients with different textures and flavors add variety. Typical mixes with chocolate candies and nuts can run 250-350 calories per ½ cup. Keep the calories down with these combos.

✗ Skip It
Peanut Butter, Nuts & Candy

Peanut butter, peanuts, and chocolate candies add fat and calories to 2 cups of Honey Nut™ and Chocolate Chex™ + 1 cup of Banana Nut Cheerios®.

230 calories, 5g sat fat, 210mg sodium

NUTRITION ALERT *Fiber*

Each of these mixes uses a whole grain as its base, which gives ½ cup up to 2 to 3g of fiber—amazing for a snack and perfect for beating that late-afternoon slump and holding you over until dinnertime.

✔ **Choose It** Fruity Crunch

3 cups Triscuit™ whole-wheat thin crisps + 1½ cups Post® Honey Nut shredded wheat + 1 cup dried man-goes + 1 cup dried apricots + ½ cup roasted almonds + ½ cup chocolate chips

Per ½ cup serving = 204 calories, 1.8g sat fat, 124mg sodium, 3.9g fiber

lose it!
26
CALORIES SAVED

✔ **Choose It** Cheese Lover's

2 cups whole-grain cheddar Goldfish® + 2½ cups cheddar-flavored mini pretzel twists + 1 cup dried apple rings + ½ cup roasted unsalted peanuts + ½ cup pecan halves

Per ½ cup serving = 126 calories, 1g sat fat, 101mg sodium, 2.1g fiber

lose it!
104
CALORIES SAVED

✔ **Choose It** Super Crunch

2 cups whole-grain Rice Chex™ + 3 cups Kashi® GoLean Crunch!® cereal + ½ cup roasted unsalted pistachios + ½ cup dried cherries

Per ½ cup serving = 116 calories, 0.3g sat fat, 68mg sodium, 3g fiber

lose it!
111
CALORIES SAVED

NUTS

Nuts are a smart snack choice with heart-healthy fats that can help lower cholesterol. They're also jam-packed with nutrients, including protein, vitamin E, folate, and magnesium, but calories can add up quickly. Downsize your portion with these mix-ins.

 NUTRITION ALERT *Sugar & Salt*

Even though nuts are healthy, they can be high in salt: One ounce of salted mixed nuts can contain almost 200mg sodium, so it's best to stick with the plain, unsalted varieties which have virtually none. And skip the sugar-coated nuts: Just one serving (about 30 nuts) can have 15g of sugar per ounce.

 RIGHT-SIZE-IT *Proper Portion*

Estimating portion sizes can be tricky, particularly with foods like nuts which vary in size. A quick tip: An ounce of nuts fits neatly into most shot glasses.

✗ *Skip It* Chocolate-Cherry Crunch

¹/₄ cup walnuts + 1 teaspoon dried cherries + 1 teaspoon dark chocolate chips

296 calories, 4.8g sat fat, 7mg sodium

✔ *Choose It* Sweet Peanut

¹/₄ cup peanuts + 1 teaspoon raisins + 1 teaspoon dried apple

258 calories, 1.4g sat fat, 188mg sodium

✔ *Choose It* Pistachio Crunch

¹/₄ cup pistachios + 1 teaspoon chopped dried apricots

191 calories, 1.5g sat fat, 166mg sodium

161

CRACKERS

Crackers can be paired with an endless variety of toppings. Whole-grain crackers are even more filling since whole grains won't cause your blood sugar levels to spike then drop. One serving—about 5 crackers—runs 80 to 130 calories, depending on the size.

✘ Skip It
Puttin' on the Ritz

5 Ritz crackers + 2 (1-ounce) slices sharp cheddar cheese divided into five squares

306 calories, 12.9g sat fat, 483mg sodium

 SHOP SMART *The Best Cracker*

Just because the package says "wheat" doesn't mean the crackers are made with whole-wheat flour. How to tell? Look at the ingredients list and make sure that "whole-wheat flour," "whole grain," "whole oats," or "whole rye" (instead of "enriched") is included and comes first or at least very close to the beginning of the list.

✔ Choose It
Strawberry-Hazelnut Graham Cracker

1 whole-wheat graham cracker sheet + 2 teaspoons chocolate-hazelnut spread + 1/4 cup sliced strawberries

135 calories, 1.4g sat fat, 72mg sodium

lose it!
171
CALORIES SAVED

✔ Choose It
PB & J

2 graham cracker sheets + 1 tablespoon peanut butter + 1 tablespoon strawberry preserves

223 calories, 2.1g sat fat, 207mg sodium

lose it!
83
CALORIES SAVED

✔ Choose It
Apple & Brie

5 Back to Nature® Harvest Whole-Wheat Crackers + 1/2 ounce Brie + 1/2 thinly sliced apple

210 calories, 2.5g sat fat, 240mg sodium

lose it!
96
CALORIES SAVED

✔ Choose It
Creamy Herb

5 Ak-Mak® Whole-Wheat Stone Ground Sesame Crackers + 2 wedges garlic-and-herb spreadable cheese

168 calories, 2.5g sat fat, 542mg sodium

lose it!
138
CALORIES SAVED

DIPS

Dips are a popular party pleaser, and they can certainly be part of a healthy snack. Done right, they're a delicious pairing for vegetables or fruit and can add a hit of calcium to your daily diet. But don't let their creamy ingredients ruin their good-for-you potential. Sub in nonfat Greek yogurt, reduced-fat sour cream, and light mayo when possible.

✖ Skip It

French Onion Dip

This creamy dip is a picnic and party staple. It pairs perfectly with crunchy, salty chips, but it's also quite hefty and high in sodium even before you add the chips.

3½ tablespoons = 105 calories, 0.9g sat fat, 368mg sodium

SHOP SMART

Chips

What's a dip without a chip? Baked and light varieties can be healthier options, but one serving of a "regular" chip won't sabotage a healthy diet. A 1-ounce serving of regular plain potato chips (about 14 to 21 chips), contains about 150 calories, 1g sat fat, and 180mg sodium. Most chips are also trans fat–free since they're cooked in vegetable oil. Corn chips are also a good alternative. Look for those that list whole corn as their first ingredient.

✔ *Choose It*
Feta-Mint Dip

Rich Greek yogurt provides creaminess for fewer calories.

ACTIVE 30 MINUTES | TOTAL 1 HOUR

1 cup plain 2% reduced-fat Greek yogurt
½ cup (2 ounces) crumbled feta cheese
½ cup finely chopped English cucumber
3 tablespoons chopped fresh mint
2 tablespoons sliced green onions
½ teaspoon freshly ground black pepper
½ teaspoon grated lemon rind
⅛ teaspoon salt
Freshly ground black pepper (optional)
Garnish: mint leaves, grated lemon rind
8 mini whole-wheat pitas, cut into 4 wedges each

PREPARATION

Place yogurt and feta in a food processor; process until smooth. Transfer to a small bowl. Stir in cucumber and next 5 ingredients (through salt). Sprinkle with additional black pepper and garnish, if desired. Serve with pita wedges. Serves 8 (serving size: 3½ tablespoons dip and 4 pita wedges)

Per serving: 66 calories, 1.4g sat fat, 172mg sodium

lose it!
39
CALORIES SAVED

 NUTRITION ALERT *Hummus*

Hummus, which is pureed chickpeas mixed with tahini (sesame seed paste), makes an incredibly nutritious and delicious dip. Two tablespoons has 54 calories, 0.4g sat fat, 72mg sodium.

CHOCOLATE CHIP COOKIES

While it's true that, in all its gooey deliciousness, a chocolate chip cookie isn't a huge nutritional offender (depending on the recipe you use), the problem is stopping at just one. This cookie recipe makeover delivers all the buttery richness at less than half the calories.

✖ Skip It

Ultimate Chocolate Chip Cookie

The classic recipe uses a good bit of butter and sugar and a good sprinkling of chocolate chips—not including some other favorite mix-ins that often make appearances like toffee, peanut butter, nuts, or sweetened coconut flakes. And cookies are another area where portion sizes are all over the map.

445 calories, 12.5g sat fat, 350mg sodium

SHOP SMART *Packaged Cookies*

There's a dizzying—and tempting—array of cookies available these days, and some are definitely healthier than others. In general, the shorter the ingredients list, the better. Besides avoiding trans fat, skip cookies that contain partially hydrogenated oils; you also want to watch out for saturated fat and sugar. Choose cookies with 2.5g saturated fat or less per cookie. And remember, moderation is key.

✔ Choose It
Browned Butter–Chocolate Chip Cookies

These guiltless cookies deliver fantastic chocolate flavor. The butter moves from nutty and brown to burned quickly, so be sure to take the pan off the heat once the butter turns amber-brown.

lose it!
349
CALORIES SAVED

ACTIVE 17 MINUTES | TOTAL 42 MINUTES

6 tablespoons unsalted butter

2 tablespoons canola oil

5.6 ounces all-purpose flour (about 1¼ cups)

3.3 ounces whole-wheat flour (about ¾ cup)

1 teaspoon baking powder

½ teaspoon kosher salt

¾ cup packed light brown sugar

⅔ cup granulated sugar

½ teaspoon vanilla extract

2 large eggs, lightly beaten

½ cup semisweet chocolate chips

⅓ cup dark chocolate chips (such as Hershey's Special Dark)

PREPARATION

Preheat oven to 375°. Heat butter in a small saucepan over medium heat; cook 5 minutes or until browned. Remove from heat; add oil. Weigh or lightly spoon flours into dry measuring cups; level with a knife. Combine flours, baking powder, and salt, stirring with a whisk. Place butter mixture and sugars in a large bowl; beat with a mixer at medium speed until combined. Add vanilla and eggs; beat until well blended. Add flour mixture, beating at low speed just until combined. Stir in chocolate chips. Drop by level tablespoonfuls 2 inches apart onto baking sheets lined with parchment paper. Bake 12 minutes at 375° or until bottoms of cookies just begin to brown. Cool slightly. Serves 40 (serving size: 1 cookie)

Per serving: 96 calories, 2g sat fat, 42mg sodium

POPCORN

Popcorn is a super-healthy snack for many reasons. First, it's a whole grain—3½ cups gives you one daily serving. Second, popcorn is a "high-volume" food, which means you get a lot of bulk for its calories: 3½ cups of air-popped runs just 108 calories and 0.2g sat fat.

 SHOP SMART *Packaged Popcorn*

The healthiest popcorn is air-popped, but read labels carefully to make sure the calorie and fat counts are low. When it comes to microwave popcorn, avoid the full-fat versions: They contain 4.5g saturated fat and trans fat combined, which can be a significant chunk of your daily limit. Stick with the 94% fat-free versions; they're nearly as good as air-popped.

✗ Skip It
Buttered Popcorn
3¹/₂ cups air-popped popcorn + 2 tablespoons melted butter + ¹/₄ teaspoon salt

312 calories, 14.8g sat fat, 786mg sodium

✔ Choose It
Sweet & Spicy
3¹/₂ cups air-popped popcorn + ¹/₂ ounce melted dark chocolate + 1 teaspoon ancho chile powder

179 calories, 2.9g sat fat, 82mg sodium

lose it!
133
CALORIES SAVED

✔ Choose It
Rosemary & Olive Oil
3¹/₂ cups air-popped popcorn + 1 teaspoon rosemary + 2 teaspoons olive oil

192 calories, 1.5g sat fat, 3mg sodium

lose it!
120
CALORIES SAVED

✔ Choose It
Cheesy Pop
3¹/₂ cups air-popped popcorn + 2 tablespoons grated Parmesan cheese + 1 teaspoon thyme

153 calories, 1.9g sat fat, 154mg sodium

lose it!
158
CALORIES SAVED

ON-THE-GO SNACKS

When you're out and about, it can be challenging to eat healthy. But there are good-for-you options in the snack aisle. Look for protein and fiber to tide you over until dinnertime. And read labels carefully: One container or bag of snacks can contain several servings.

lose it!
70
CALORIES SAVED

✘ Skip It
Snickers®
250 calories, 4.5g sat fat, 120mg sodium, 27g sugar

✔ Choose It
Clif Mojo® Dark Chocolate Cherry Almond Trail Mix Bar
180 calories, 2.5g sat fat, 120mg sodium, 13g sugar

 SHOP SMART *Granola Bars*

Granola definitely has a health-food halo, but when you're in the market for bars, keep these guidelines in mind.
- The first ingredient should be a whole grain, like oats.
- One bar should have 200 calories or less, less than 6g total fat, and 5 to 10g protein.
- Watch out for "natural" sugar. Whether it's made with agave, brown rice syrup, or organic evaporated cane juice, you should choose bars that have the least amount of the sweet stuff.

Two More Granola Bar Favorites
- Kashi® TLC Trail Mix Chewy Granola Bar: 140 calories, 0.5g sat fat, 95mg sodium
- Nature Valley® Roasted Nut Crunch Almond Crunch Bar: 190 calories, 1.5g sat fat, 180mg sodium

✖ Skip It
Plain M&M's®

(1 bag)

240 calories, 6g sat fat, 30mg sodium, 30g sugar

✖ Skip It
Trail Mix

(6 tablespoons)

280 calories, 0g sat fat, 70mg sodium, 22g sugar

✖ Skip It
Packaged Raisin Bran Muffin

460 calories, 3g sat fat, 450mg sodium

lose it!
90 CALORIES SAVED

✔ Choose It
Pretzel M&M's

(1 bag)

150 calories, 3g sat fat, 120mg sodium, 17g sugar

lose it!
140 CALORIES SAVED

✔ Choose It
Nature Valley® Dark Chocolate & Nut Chewy Trail Mix Bar

140 calories, 1g sat fat, 65mg sodium, 12g sugar

lose it!
220 CALORIES SAVED

✔ Choose It
Honey Nut Chex Mix®

(1 cup)

240 calories, 1g sat fat, 270mg sodium, 10g sugar

YOGURT

Yogurt is an inherently healthy snack: One cup not only boasts one-third of your daily calcium needs, but also the protein and other minerals that keep your bones and muscles strong. With endless options to choose from—including yogurts made from soy, almond, and coconut milk—it can be a challenge to navigate the yogurt aisle.

✖ Skip It
Fruit-flavored Yogurt

Often yogurts that are fruit-flavored don't contain any real fruit, but instead a sugary mixture that can include high-fructose corn syrup. One 6-ounce container of fruit-flavored yogurt can contain more than 25g sugar—that's more than the sugar in two Oreos®!

(One 6-ounce container)
180 calories, 1.5g sat fat, 110mg sodium, 28g sugar

NUTRITION ALERT

Good Bacteria

A healthy digestive system has the right levels of "good" bacteria to help keep things running smoothly, and yogurt can help you get your fill. The FDA requires all yogurts to include at least two strains of bacteria, *L.bulgaricus* and *S. thermophilus*, but manufacturers can add more. The National Yogurt Association seal ensures that the yogurt contains enough cultures to make a difference.

lose it!
80
CALORIES SAVED

lose it!
100
CALORIES SAVED

✔ *Choose It*
Plain Low-fat Yogurt

Plain, low-fat yogurt gives you a blank slate to customize and add nutritious, low-calorie, low-fat mix-ins. Even though yogurt is high in protein, it's pretty low in fiber, so pairing one container with ½ cup of fruit—blueberries, raspberries, or chopped pineapple—will add a shot of fiber. That's a much healthier way to get your fruit fix than relying on fruit-flavored yogurts.

(One 6-ounce container)
100 calories, 1.5g sat fat, 115mg sodium, 12g sugar

✔ *Choose It*
Low-fat or Fat-free Greek Yogurt

Greek yogurt may not be all that much lower in calories than regular low-fat yogurt, but the major benefit is the higher level of protein, which means you'll feel full on fewer calories. What's behind the protein power? Strained yogurts like Greek require three to four times more milk to produce than regular yogurt. As with regular yogurts, it's best to go with the low-fat or fat-free plain variety—otherwise you could be getting as much as 11g sat fat.

(One 6-ounce container)
80 calories, 0g sat fat, 50mg sodium, 6g sugar

YOGURT PARFAITS

A parfait is a great way to jazz up yogurt. The cool, creamy texture is an ideal base for toppings like sweet fruits and crunchy nuts, which create a delicious contrast. A ½-cup serving of low-fat yogurt is a good starting point for a topping of fresh berries, dried fruit, or toasted nuts.

 NUTRITION ALERT Go Greek

Yogurt's a great way to get bone-strengthening calcium and filling protein, and Greek yogurt is the super-star of this dairy bunch: One serving has 7 more grams of protein and half the sodium of regular fat-free yogurt. When it comes to other types, watch out for sugar: More than 25g sugar per serving may mean added (and unnecessary) calories.

✗ *Skip It*
Peanut Butter and Nuts

½ cup plain Greek yogurt + 2 tablespoons chocolate syrup + 2 tablespoons peanut butter + 2 tablespoons chopped walnuts = 534 calories, 13.3g sat fat, 195mg sodium

534 CALORIES

lose it!
280 CALORIES SAVED

✔ **Choose It** Peachy Coconut
½ cup organic vanilla low-fat yogurt + ½ cup fresh chopped peaches + 2 tablespoons shredded coconut + 1 tablespoon chopped unsalted cashews = 254 calories, 8.1g sat fat, 55mg sodium

lose it!
310 CALORIES SAVED

✔ **Choose It** Nutty Honey
½ cup plain low-fat yogurt + ½ cup blueberries + 1 tablespoon honey + 2 tablespoons chopped pecans = 224 calories, 1.7g sat fat, 87mg sodium

FROZEN YOGURT

Frozen yogurt can be a healthy dessert as long as you don't serve yourself a mountain's worth with toppings. Start with ½ cup (about 3½ ounces), which has approximately 80 to 120 calories, depending on the flavor you choose. You also get good-for-you protein and calcium.

 RIGHT-SIZE-IT

Super Scoops

Because of frozen yogurt's creamy deliciousness, it can be too easy to serve yourself too much. A good way to limit your portions is to use an ice cream scooper—two scoops from most equal ½ cup—or use a small bowl so you'll naturally take less.

✘ *Skip It*
Fudge Toffee

2 tablespoons crushed toffee + 2 tablespoons hot fudge sauce + 2 tablespoons rainbow sprinkles

400 calories, 9g sat fat, 190mg sodium

✔ *Choose It*
Candy Bar Crunch

1 tablespoon crumbled Kit Kat + 1 tablespoon chocolate-covered raisins + 1 tablespoon crushed Butterfinger®

151 calories, 4.5g sat fat, 39mg sodium

lose it!
249
CALORIES SAVED

✔ *Choose It*
Banana-Nut

¹/₄ cup banana slices + 1 tablespoon walnuts + 1 tablespoon semisweet chocolate chips

132 calories, 2.4g sat fat, 2mg sodium

lose it!
268
CALORIES SAVED

✔ *Choose It*
Choco-Peanut

1 tablespoon peanuts + 1 tablespoon chocolate chips

110 calories, 2.6g sat fat, 9mg sodium

lose it!
290
CALORIES SAVED

ICE CREAM

Ice cream can be an indulgence, but having a reasonable serving of a full-fat version of this treat doesn't do that much damage. Slimmed-down versions leave more room for toppings and can be a great source of calcium—¹/₂ cup contains 10 to 15% of your daily needs.

✗ Skip It
Regular Full-fat Ice Cream

"Real" ice cream is most definitely a splurge, but calorie and fat counts can vary widely from brand to brand. A lot of that depends on what mix-ins the ice creams contain. For example, ¹/₂ cup of a chocolate chip cookie dough or fudge chunk ice cream can pack up to 300 calories and 20 grams of fat! The good news is that plain ice cream only contains about 140 to 160 calories and 2 to 5 grams of saturated fat in a ¹/₂-cup serving.

270 calories, 11g sat fat, 21g sugar

 **NUTRITION ALERT**

Sugar Alcohols

If an ice cream is labeled sugar free or low carb, this often means they contain sugar alcohols—mannitol, sorbitol, xylitol, isomalt, maltitol, and hydrogenated starch hydrolysates. As sugar substitutes, they add fewer calories. But be aware that they can have side effects, including bloating and stomach upset when eaten in large amounts.

 SHOP SMART *Label Lingo*

Browse the freezer aisle, and you'll see several terms on lighter ice cream. Here's what they technically mean:

- **Low-fat:** A ¹/₂-cup serving must contain no more than 3g total fat.
- **Reduced-fat:** Contains 25% less total fat than a brand's original. This doesn't always mean that it's the lowest-fat option. Why? The more fat in the original version, the more fat in the reduced-fat type.
- **Light:** A light ice cream can contain either 50% less fat or 33% fewer total calories than the original. Most swap in whole or low-fat milk for the cream to lower the count.
- **Fat-free:** A fat-free ice cream can have up to 0.5g fat.
- **Whipped:** Air has been added during the churning process. Total fat counts are generally 4 to 5 grams.

lose it!
109
CALORIES
SAVED

✔ *Choose It*

Homemade Vanilla Bean Ice Cream

This recipe has 75 percent less fat than regular ice cream, but it's still creamy and rich.

ACTIVE 23 MINUTES | TOTAL 4 HOURS, 30 MINUTES

- 1 cup half-and-half
- ½ cup sugar, divided
- 2 tablespoons light-colored corn syrup
- ⅛ teaspoon salt
- 1 (12-ounce) can evaporated low-fat milk
- 1 vanilla bean, split lengthwise
- 3 large egg yolks

PREPARATION

1. Combine half-and-half, ¼ cup sugar, corn syrup, salt, and evaporated milk in a medium, heavy saucepan. Scrape seeds from vanilla bean; add seeds and bean to milk mixture. Heat milk mixture to 180° or until tiny bubbles form around edge (do not boil). Remove from heat; cover and let stand 10 minutes.

2. Combine ¼ cup sugar and egg yolks in a medium bowl, stirring well with a whisk. Gradually add hot milk mixture to egg mixture, stirring constantly with a whisk. Return milk mixture to pan. Cook over medium heat until a thermometer registers 160°, stirring constantly. Remove from heat. Place pan in a large ice-filled bowl for 20 minutes or until egg mixture is cool, stirring occasionally. Pour milk mixture through a fine sieve into the freezer can of an ice-cream freezer; discard solids. Freeze according to manufacturer's instructions. Spoon ice cream into a freezer-safe container; cover and freeze 3 hours or until firm. Serves 8 (serving size: ½ cup)

Per serving: 161 calories, 3.1g sat fat, 108mg sodium

ICE CREAM SUNDAE

With fruit, nuts, and calcium-rich ice cream at their core, sundaes have the potential to add a bit of nutrition to your daily diet. But they can also easily go awry. Just make the ice cream light—or go for one scoop of the real thing—and add ingredients wisely.

 SHOP SMART *Sauces*

Caramel, chocolate, and strawberry sauces and syrups are what give an ice cream sundae its gooey deliciousness. And, in the right amounts, they're not a dish deal-breaker. Just be sure to look for those without high-fructose corn syrup. Light versions can be a good choice, but keep in mind that they often contain artificial sweeteners.

745 CALORIES

✘ *Skip It*
Super Split

2 cups vanilla ice cream + 1 sliced banana + 3 squirts whipped cream + ½ tablespoon chopped nuts + 2 tablespoons fudge sauce + 1 tablespoon caramel sauce + 3 maraschino cherries

745 calories, 16.7g sat fat, 195mg sodium

lose it!
305 CALORIES SAVED

✔ *Choose It* Caramel Apple

1 cup vanilla ice cream + 2 tablespoons fat-free caramel apple dip (such as Marzetti®)

440 calories, 9g sat fat, 240mg sodium

lose it!
468 CALORIES SAVED

✔ *Choose It* Chocolate Turtle

½ cup light chocolate ice cream + 1 scoop fat-free vanilla ice cream + 1½ tablespoons fat-free caramel syrup (such as Smucker's®) + 1 teaspoon chopped pecans

277 calories, 4.2g sat fat, 101mg sodium

FROZEN DESSERTS

You might be surprised to learn that calorie and fat counts for all varieties of ice cream—regular and light—can differ widely among brands. For some, the full-fat version comes close to the calorie and fat count of a lightened version.

lose it!
60
CALORIES SAVED

✖ *Skip It*
Häagen-Dazs® Vanilla Low Fat Frozen Yogurt *(½ cup)*

170 calories, 1g sat fat, 45mg sodium, 21g sugar

✔ *Choose It*
Häagen-Dazs Raspberry Sorbet *(½ cup)*

110 calories, 0g sat fat, 0mg sodium, 25g sugar

 SHOP SMART *Sorbet vs. Sherbet*

Sorbet is a combination of fruit, juice, and water. It's naturally fat-free and about 120 calories per ½-cup serving. Sherbet is made with fruit, juice, water, milk, egg whites, or gelatin and runs about 160 calories per ½ cup. Both are great swaps for ice cream, but these frozen treats don't have the calcium and protein found in frozen yogurt.

 SHOP SMART *Dairy Alternatives*

Ice creams made with soy, almond, and rice milk are a great option for the lactose-intolerant. But just because they don't contain cream or whole milk doesn't mean they're lighter: Many can contain just as much—or more—calories and fat as regular ice cream, so read labels carefully.

✖ *Skip It*

Häagen-Dazs Pineapple Coconut Ice Cream

(½ cup)

230 calories, 8g sat fat, 40mg sodium, 23g sugar

✖ *Skip It*

Häagen-Dazs Chocolate Ice Cream

(½ cup)

260 calories, 10g sat fat, 45mg sodium, 19g sugar

✖ *Skip It*

Ben & Jerry's® Cookie Dough Ice Cream

(½ cup)

280 calories, 9g sat fat, 75mg sodium, 25g sugar

lose it!
110 CALORIES SAVED

✔ *Choose It*

Häagen-Dazs Lemon Sorbet

(½ cup)

120 calories, 0g sat fat, 0mg sodium, 27g sugar

lose it!
120 CALORIES SAVED

✔ *Choose It*

Breyers® Chocolate Ice Cream

(½ cup)

140 calories, 4.5g sat fat, 45mg sodium, 16g sugar

lose it!
150 CALORIES SAVED

✔ *Choose It*

Edy's® Slow-Churned® Cookie Dough Ice Cream

(½ cup)

130 calories, 2g sat fat, 50mg sodium, 14g sugar

FROZEN DESSERTS

Overall, frozen treats like ice-cream bars, sandwiches, and pre-assembled cones don't end up costing you too many calories since they're pretty compact and have the advantage of built-in portion control. Plus, there are lots of delicious light versions available.

lose it!
110
CALORIES SAVED

✗ Skip It
Klondike® Choco Taco®
240 calories, 9g sat fat, 110mg sodium, 20g sugar

✔ Choose It
Weight Watchers® Smart Ones®
Peanut Butter Cup Sundae
130 calories, 1.5g sat fat, 55mg sodium, 13g sugar

 SHOP SMART *Look for Light*
Many brands, including Good Humor® and Klondike, make lighter versions of their original products. Klondike for example, has an entire line of 100-calorie treats, including ice-cream bars, sandwiches, and pops.

✘ *Skip It*

Fat Boy® Cookies 'n' Cream Ice Cream Sandwich

220 calories, 5g sat fat, 160mg sodium, 19g sugar

✘ *Skip It*

Dark Magnum® Bar

240 calories, 11g sat fat, 40mg sodium, 18g sugar

✘ *Skip It*

Ben & Jerry's® Chubby Hubby® Ice Cream

(½ cup)

340 calories, 11g sat fat, 150mg sodium, 25g sugar

lose it!
70
CALORIES SAVED

✔ *Choose It*

Skinny Cow® Vanilla Caramel Cone

150 calories, 2g sat fat, 80mg sodium, 17g sugar

lose it!
140
CALORIES SAVED

✔ *Choose It*

Popsicle® Original Fudge Bar

100 calories, 1g sat fat, 80mg sodium, 14g sugar

lose it!
220
CALORIES SAVED

✔ *Choose It*

Edy's® Slow-Churned® Nestlé® Drumstick® Sundae Cone

(½ cup)

120 calories, 2g sat fat, 40mg sodium, 14g sugar

BANANA BREAD

You can enjoy banana bread for dessert, breakfast, or a snack. Mix-ins like walnuts and flaxseed can up the heart-healthy value by adding a dose of omega-3 fatty acids and a bit of fiber. Banana bread freezes well, so bake a few loaves at a time; make the glaze before serving.

✗ Skip It

Classic Banana Bread

Traditional banana bread recipes use a good bit of butter and sugar to make the loaf moist and tender. Added extras like nuts or bits of chocolate and a thick glaze can ramp up calories if they're not added in smart amounts.

283 calories, 6g sat fat, 291mg sodium

 SHOP SMART

The Best Bananas

The perfect bananas for banana bread don't look so perfect. They should be very ripe, almost black, or very speckled. It takes a week or more to go from green to banana-bread ready. To hasten ripening, place them in a paper bag with a bruised apple, which produces ethylene gas that helps speed the process. Once ripe, refrigerate or freeze unpeeled bananas in zip-top freezer bags; thaw before mashing. Freezing mashed bananas doesn't work—they're too watery and not suitable to use.

✔ *Choose It*
Basic Banana Bread

By cutting back on butter and adding flaxseed, this bread is just as satisfying as the original, but lower in calories and better for you.

ACTIVE 15 MINUTES | TOTAL 1 HOUR, 20 MINUTES

1½ cups mashed ripe banana
⅓ cup plain fat-free yogurt
5 tablespoons butter, melted
2 large eggs
½ cup granulated sugar
½ cup packed brown sugar
6.75 ounces all-purpose flour (about 1½ cups)
¼ cup ground flaxseed
¾ teaspoon baking soda
½ teaspoon salt
½ teaspoon ground cinnamon
⅛ teaspoon ground allspice
Cooking spray
⅓ cup powdered sugar
1½ teaspoons 1% low-fat milk

lose it!
116
CALORIES SAVED

PREPARATION

1. Preheat oven to 350°. Combine first 4 ingredients in a large bowl; beat with a mixer at medium speed. Add granulated and brown sugars; beat until combined.

2. Weigh or lightly spoon flour into dry measuring cups; level with a knife. Combine flour and next 5 ingredients (through ground allspice). Add flour mixture to banana mixture; beat just until blended. Pour batter into a 9 x 5–inch loaf pan coated with cooking spray. Bake at 350° for 55 minutes or until a wooden pick inserted in center comes out clean. Remove from oven; cool 10 minutes in pan on a wire rack. Remove bread from pan; cool completely. Combine powdered sugar and milk, stirring until smooth; drizzle over bread. Serves 16 (serving size: 1 slice)

Per serving: 167 calories, 2.5g sat fat, 173mg sodium

BROWNIES

The best brownies are fudgy, chewy, gooey, and dense. How can you achieve that with fewer calories and fat? While it is a bit tricky—using too little fat or too much flour can make the texture less than desirable—lighter and deliciously decadent brownies are possible.

✘ Skip It
Everything Brownies

Brownies are a piece of cake to make. But when they're as rich as any buttery bar cookie—and in the portions that are served at some bakeries and coffeehouses—they could put an entire family in a sugar daze with plenty of dark chocolate and tons of butter and sugar.

366 calories, 14.1g sat fat, 78mg sodium

🛒 SHOP SMART
Packaged Brownie Mixes

Mixes can be a great way to save time, but when you're selecting a brand, be sure to read ingredients lists closely to make sure "partially hydrogenated oils" aren't included. They'll add unhealthy trans fats to your baked goods. Also, when you're cooking, go for an oil that's lower in saturated fat and has a neutral flavor, such as canola.

🥄 RIGHT-SIZE-IT   *Measure Carefully*

When baking light brownies, properly measuring flour is probably the most crucial factor. The most accurate way to get the same results we do is to weigh the flour. If you don't have a kitchen scale, then be sure to lightly scoop the flour into the measuring cups and use a knife to scrape the excess off the top. Don't pack it in or tap the cup on the counter: You'll end up with baked goods that have too much flour—and are much too dry.

✔ Choose It
Classic Fudge-Walnut Brownies

The key to keeping regular brownies moist is loads of butter or other fat. In this lightened version, take care not to overbake.

lose it!
180
CALORIES SAVED

3.38 ounces all-purpose flour (about ¾ cup)

1 cup granulated sugar

¾ cup unsweetened cocoa

½ cup packed brown sugar

½ teaspoon baking powder

¼ teaspoon salt

1 cup bittersweet chocolate chunks, divided

⅓ cup fat-free milk

6 tablespoons butter, melted

1 teaspoon vanilla extract

2 large eggs, lightly beaten

½ cup chopped walnuts, divided

Cooking spray

PREPARATION

1. Preheat oven to 350°. Weigh or lightly spoon flour into dry measuring cups; level with a knife. Combine flour and next 5 ingredients (through salt) in a large bowl. Combine ½ cup chocolate and milk in a microwave-safe bowl; microwave at HIGH 1 minute, stirring after 30 seconds. Stir in butter, vanilla, and eggs. Add chocolate mixture, ½ cup chocolate, and ¼ cup nuts to flour mixture; stir to combine.

2. Pour batter into a 9-inch square metal baking pan coated with cooking spray; sprinkle with ¼ cup nuts. Bake at 350° for 22 minutes or until a wooden pick inserted in center comes out with moist crumbs clinging. Cool in pan on a wire rack. Serves 20 (serving size: 1 brownie)

Per serving: 186 calories, 4.2g sat fat, 74mg sodium

LEMON SQUARES

The meeting up of creamy, zippy citrus and nutty cookie goodness, lemon squares are refreshingly tangy and buttery-crisp. Somehow that puckery citrus makes a good lemon square seem lighter than it really is, because typical recipes can pack up to more than 300 calories in one little square.

✗ *Skip It*

Traditional Lemon Squares

These brightly flavored bars typically contain a full cup of butter and 1½ pounds of sugar—adding up to more than 400 calories per bar. Large portion sizes can also make these bars, which do taste deceptively light, tip the calorie scale.

425 calories, 11.6g sat fat, 151mg sodium

NUTRITION ALERT

Soften Butter the Right Way

Need to soften butter fast? Don't stick it in the microwave: Instead, cut the butter into tablespoon-sized portions and let them stand at room temperature for 30 to 45 minutes. Too-soft butter won't cream properly with sugar and can result in cookie dough or crust that spreads too much as it bakes.

✔ Choose It
Lighter Lemon Squares

This lighter version doesn't compromise the bright, zesty filling and the buttery, crumbly crust.

ACTIVE 15 MINUTES | TOTAL 3 HOURS

CRUST

3.4 ounces all-purpose flour (about ¾ cup)

¼ cup powdered sugar

3 tablespoons pine nuts, toasted and coarsely chopped

⅛ teaspoon salt

2 tablespoons chilled unsalted butter, cut into small pieces

2 tablespoons canola oil

Cooking spray

FILLING

¾ cup granulated sugar

2 tablespoons all-purpose flour

1 teaspoon grated lemon rind

½ cup fresh lemon juice

2 large eggs

1 large egg white

2 tablespoons powdered sugar

lose it!
301
CALORIES SAVED

PREPARATION

1. Preheat oven to 350°. To prepare crust, weigh or lightly spoon flour into dry measuring cups; level with a knife. Place flour, ¼ cup powdered sugar, pine nuts, and salt in a food processor; pulse 2 times to combine. Add butter and canola oil. Pulse 3 to 5 times or until mixture resembles coarse meal. Place mixture into the bottom of an 8-inch square glass or ceramic baking dish coated with cooking spray; press into bottom of pan. Bake at 350° for 20 minutes or until lightly browned. Reduce oven temperature to 325°.

2. To prepare filling, combine granulated sugar and next 5 ingredients (through egg white) in a medium bowl, stirring with a whisk until smooth. Pour mixture over crust. Bake at 325° for 20 minutes or until set. Remove from oven, and cool completely in pan on a wire rack. Cover and chill for at least 2 hours. Sprinkle squares evenly with 2 tablespoons powdered sugar. Serves 16 (serving size: 1 square)

Per serving: 124 calories, 1.3g sat fat, 31mg sodium

CUPCAKES

There are so many ways you can customize a cupcake to make it a flavorful indulgence. And it has the benefit of being portion-controlled—as long as you eat just one! Full-fat dairy ingredients and ample frosting can ramp up the calories and saturated fat, but there are ways to create major flavor without major calories.

✗ *Skip It*
Chocolate Cupcake

Cupcakes may be small, but they can certainly pack in a good bit of calories, thanks to a rich cake made with lots of butter and big portions of nuts, chocolate, or an assortment of other flavorings, plus a thick layer of creamy frosting and myriad other sweet garnishes and toppings.

400 calories, 11.6g sat fat, 113mg sodium

 NUTRITION ALERT *Dark Chocolate*

When eaten in moderation, dark chocolate may help lower blood pressure and reduce LDL, or "bad" cholesterol. Look for minimally processed cocoa powder and dark chocolate.

✔ *Choose It*
Chocolate Cupcakes with Vanilla Cream Cheese Frosting

This lightened version still delivers big flavor and rich texture.

ACTIVE 23 MINUTES | TOTAL 1 HOUR, 11 MINUTES

CUPCAKES

1 cup granulated sugar

½ cup egg substitute

¼ cup canola oil

½ teaspoon vanilla extract

6¾ ounces all-purpose flour (about 1½ cups)

½ cup unsweetened cocoa

1 teaspoon baking soda

1 teaspoon instant coffee granules

½ teaspoon baking powder

¼ teaspoon salt

1 cup nonfat buttermilk

FROSTING

1 cup powdered sugar

½ teaspoon vanilla extract

Dash of salt

1 (8-ounce) block ⅓-less-fat cream cheese, softened

lose it!
197
**CALORIES
SAVED**

PREPARATION

1. Preheat oven to 350°. To prepare cupcakes, place first 4 ingredients in a large bowl; beat with a mixer at medium speed until well blended (about 2 minutes). Weigh or lightly spoon flour into dry measuring cups; level with a knife. Combine flour and next 5 ingredients (through ¼ teaspoon salt), stirring well with a whisk. Stir flour mixture into sugar mixture alternately with buttermilk, beginning and ending with flour mixture; mix after each addition just until blended.

2. Place 16 paper muffin cup liners in muffin cups; spoon about 2½ tablespoons batter into each cup. Bake at 350° for 18 minutes or until a wooden pick inserted in center of a cupcake comes out with moist crumbs attached (do not overbake). Remove cupcakes from pans; cool on a wire rack.

3. To prepare frosting, combine powdered sugar and remaining ingredients in a medium bowl. Beat with a mixer at medium speed until combined. Increase speed to medium-high, and beat until smooth. Spread about 1 tablespoon frosting on top of each cupcake. Serves 16 (serving size: 1 cupcake)

Per serving: 203 calories, 2.1g sat fat, 211mg sodium

CARROT CAKE

When it comes to traditional desserts, you might think a lighter version just isn't realistic, but it is possible to make a few small tweaks and still come out with the same delicious, indulgent treat. Skip extra calories and fat, but not the flavor with this recipe.

✗ Skip It
Traditional Carrot Cake

Carrot cake may sound like a healthier option, but it's actually a calorie and fat disaster. A three-layer cake recipe uses 1½ cups of oil, is frosted with one stick of butter and a whole pound of cream cheese, and is a pecan extravaganza. The calories and sat fat show it.

1,045 calories, 18g sat fat, 766mg sodium

 NUTRITION ALERT *Build a Better Cake*

A lighter and just-as-delicious cake strikes a balance between these ingredients:
• Flour: It's the framework for a cake, giving it structure and texture. Using the right amount is crucial, particularly in lightened recipes, so weigh and measure it carefully.
• Sugar: Granulated and brown sugars often team up to round out other flavors.
• Butter: Always use the real thing (just less) since it's key to texture and taste.

✔ *Choose It*
Carrot Cake

This tender cake is packed with grated carrot, flaked coconut, chopped pecans, and, just like the traditional version, a thick cream cheese frosting.

ACTIVE 15 MINUTES | TOTAL 1 HOUR, 20 MINUTES

- **6.75 ounces all-purpose flour (about 1½ cups)**
- 1⅓ cups granulated sugar
- ½ cup sweetened flaked coconut
- ⅓ cup chopped pecans
- 2 teaspoons baking soda
- 1 teaspoon salt
- 2 teaspoons ground cinnamon
- 3 tablespoons canola oil
- 2 large eggs
- 2 cups grated carrots
- 1½ cups canned, drained, crushed pineapple
- **Cooking spray**
- 2 tablespoons softened butter
- 1 (8-ounce) block ⅓-less-fat cream cheese, softened
- 3 cups powdered sugar
- 2 teaspoons vanilla extract

lose it!
723
CALORIES SAVED

PREPARATION

1. Preheat oven to 350°. Weigh or lightly spoon flour into dry measuring cups; level with a knife. Combine flour, granulated sugar, coconut, pecans, baking soda, salt, and ground cinnamon in a large bowl; whisk well. Combine canola oil and eggs; stir well. Stir egg mixture, grated carrots, and pineapple into flour mixture.

2. Spoon batter into a 13 x 9–inch metal baking pan coated with cooking spray. Bake at 350° for 35 minutes or until a wooden pick inserted in center comes out clean. Cool completely on a wire rack.

3. Combine butter and cream cheese in a bowl. Beat with a mixer at medium speed until smooth. Beat in powdered sugar and vanilla just until smooth. Spread frosting over top of cake. Serves 16 (serving size: 1 square)

Per serving: 322 calories, 4.2g sat fat, 403mg sodium

195

KEY LIME PIE

There's an addictive quality to Key lime pie's finely tuned balance of the sweet and the tart, the creamy and the crunchy, all crowned with fluffy cream. It seems so airy, but it's more than 500 calories of airy. Time for a makeover, indeed.

✗ Skip It
Classic Key Lime Pie

This may have seemed like a light, ethereal pie all along, but tastes are sometimes deceiving. Butter in the crust and full-fat sweetened condensed milk in the filling plus a top layer of whipped cream can cause the calories to add up to over 500 calories per slice.

519 calories, 19.6g sat fat, 252mg sodium

 SHOP SMART

Ready-Made Crusts
Your main concern with store-bought pie crusts is trans fats: Read ingredients lists carefully and skip those that list "partially hydrogenated oil." Here's the rub: Most mainstream brands do contain trans fats, so you may have to search out lesser-known options—or make your own.

 NUTRITION ALERT

That Has How Much Fat?!
You may see individually wrapped, one-serving pies and think, "Oh, good, automatic portion control." Well, they're anything but. One "snack-sized" pie can pack in as much as 450 calories and 14g saturated fat.

✔ *Choose It*
Key Lime Pie

The breakthrough discovery of this pie is using white chocolate in the crust. It melts in the oven to bind the crumbs, and then hardens when cooled to form a perfectly crisp crust (with fewer calories than a traditional, butter-laced crust).

ACTIVE 25 MINUTES | TOTAL 3 HOURS, 4 MINUTES

CRUST

1 cup graham cracker crumbs

1 tablespoon brown sugar

⅛ teaspoon salt

1 ounce premium white chocolate, grated or finely chopped

2 tablespoons butter, melted and cooled

1 tablespoon canola oil

Cooking spray

FILLING

½ cup plain 2% reduced-fat Greek yogurt

½ teaspoon grated lime rind

½ cup fresh Key lime juice or fresh lime juice

3 large egg yolks

1 (14-ounce) can fat-free sweetened condensed milk

¾ cup frozen fat-free whipped topping, thawed

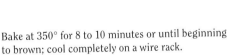

lose it!
239
CALORIES SAVED

PREPARATION

1. Preheat oven to 350°. To prepare crust, combine crumbs, sugar, salt, and chocolate in a bowl, stirring well to combine. Add butter and oil; toss with a fork until moist. Press crumb mixture into bottom and up sides of a 9-inch pie plate coated with cooking spray.

Bake at 350° for 8 to 10 minutes or until beginning to brown; cool completely on a wire rack.

2. To prepare filling, place yogurt and next 4 ingredients (through milk) in a bowl; beat with a mixer at medium speed 2 minutes. Pour mixture into prepared crust. Bake at 350° for 14 minutes or until set. Cool pie completely on a wire rack. Cover loosely, and chill at least 2 hours. Serve with whipped topping. Serves 8 (serving size: 1 slice)

Per serving: 280 calories, 3.6g sat fat, 147mg sodium

CHEESECAKE

Think there's no way to make this creamy dessert lighter without sacrificing taste? False. We start with a traditional cheesecake recipe, and then swap in lower-fat and -calorie ingredients to improve its nutrition profile without compromising melt-in-your-mouth texture or flavor.

✗ Skip It

Classic Cheesecake

Traditional cheesecakes run the calorie gamut. Gargantuan portions; a thick layer of filling made with full-fat cream cheese, egg yolks, and sugar, and rich crusts; myriad stir-ins and toppings can amp up the calorie load even higher, tipping the scales at more than 1,300 calories *per slice*. But a standard no-frills cheesecake will still pack a punch.

678 calories, 30.5g sat fat, 436mg sodium

 NUTRITION ALERT

Choosing Cream Cheese

Combining fat-free cream cheese with ⅓-less-fat cheese is a great way to lighten the calorie load without sacrificing a creamy texture. However, avoid the temptation to use all fat-free cream cheese to cut calories even more. The texture won't be as rich (or satisfying), and the cheesecake won't set properly or become firm in the center.

✔ Choose It
Light Cheesecake

One-third-less-fat cream cheese can do wonders to lower calories without compromising flavor. Mixing the ⅓-less-fat cheese with fat-free cream cheese and light sour cream helps reduce the sat fat and calories even more while still retaining a luscious, creamy, satisfying texture. A slightly reduced portion size also helps keep this dessert in check.

ACTIVE 13 MINUTES | TOTAL 10 HOURS, 45 MINUTES

10 sheets graham crackers

1¼ cups granulated sugar, divided

4 tablespoons butter, melted and cooled

Cooking spray

2 (8-ounce) packages ⅓-less-fat cream cheese, softened

1 (8-ounce) package fat-free cream cheese, softened

½ cup light sour cream

3 tablespoons all-purpose flour

3 large eggs

1 teaspoon vanilla extract

lose it!
407
CALORIES
SAVED

PREPARATION

1. Preheat oven to 350°. Place graham crackers and ¼ cup granulated sugar in a food processer; process until finely ground. Transfer to a bowl; add melted butter, stirring until well blended. Firmly press mixture into bottom and 1 inch up sides of a 9-inch springform pan coated with cooking spray. Bake at 350° for 10 minutes or until golden brown. Cool. Reduce oven temperature to 325°.

2. Place cream cheeses and sour cream in a large bowl; beat with a mixer at medium speed until smooth and fluffy. Add 1 cup granulated sugar and the flour; beat well. Add eggs, one at a time, beating well after each. Stir in vanilla extract.

3. Pour cheese mixture into prepared crust; bake at 325° for 37 minutes or until cheesecake center barely moves when pan is touched. Turn oven off. Leave cheesecake in oven with door partially open 1 hour. Remove cheesecake from oven; run knife around outside edge. Cool completely on a wire rack. Cover and chill at least 8 hours. Serves 14 (serving size: 1 slice)

Per serving: 271 calories, 7.7g sat fat, 342mg sodium

APPLEBEE'S℠

Applebee's has a delicious-sounding roster of rich, decadent desserts—many of which involve chocolate—making them hard to resist. But the good news is there are a few options that won't break your calorie bank.

lose it!
1,230
CALORIES SAVED

✘ Skip It
Blue Ribbon Brownie

Complete with hunks of dark chocolate, nuts, hot fudge, and two scoops of vanilla ice cream, this brownie's more like a brownie and hot fudge sundae rolled into one. Yes, it's perfect for sharing, but you'd have to split it with at least five people to make a real dent in the calorie count.

1,600 calories, 41g sat fat, 910mg sodium

✔ Choose It
Brownie Bite

This is what dessert should look like: Still plenty of chocolaty richness with nuts and hot fudge sauce paired with vanilla ice cream, but in a reasonably sized portion. Skip appetizers and calorie-heavy drinks to keep this on your menu.

370 calories, 10g sat fat, 210mg sodium

 ORDER SMART *Shooters*

It's a clever portion control package: Applebee's "dessert shooters" are desserts served in a shot glass. Fun and lower in calories and fat, too.

DAIRY QUEEN®

A true banana split and a hot fudge sundae aren't awful nutritional choices when portions are kept in check, but many ice-cream shops and restaurants go overboard with gargantuan servings. The basic ingredients are often rich and can be entirely satisfying in smaller portions.

lose it!
420
CALORIES SAVED

✗ Skip It
Turtle Waffle Bowl Sundae

A mountain of ice cream, caramel sauce, and a chocolate-dipped waffle cone bowl.

810 calories, 18g sat fat, 320mg sodium, 76g sugar

✓ Choose It
Peanut Butter Sundae *(small)*

A generous serving of vanilla soft-serve topped with a peanut butter sauce is the way to go. The peanut butter contrasted with the sweet ice cream gives this sundae enough flavor so you don't need more toppings. And there's a lot less sugar, too.

390 calories, 7g sat fat, 260mg sodium, 28g sugar

 ORDER SMART *Simple Sundaes*

DQ's basic sundaes are a smart way to satisfy your sweet tooth. A small cup filled with vanilla soft-serve and topped with your choice of one sauce will keep the calories down. Choose caramel or strawberry and it will run 300 calories or less.

DAIRY QUEEN®

*A whirlwind of ice cream mixed with cookie, candy, and/or fruit bits, the DQ Blizzard® packs
a sweet and creamy punch, but certain flavors are more caloric than others. If you're going to
splurge on this, be sure to share it, or eat less the rest of the day: Even the small is 500+ calories.*

lose it!
90
CALORIES SAVED

✘ *Skip It*
Cookie Dough Blizzard *(small)*
710 calories, 16g sat fat, 400mg sodium, 75g sugar

✔ *Choose It*
Oreo® Cookies Blizzard *(small)*
620 calories, 11g sat fat, 500mg sodium, 67g sugar

NUTRITION ALERT

That Has How Many Calories?!

Beware the large Blizzard: It packs a snowstorm of calories and fat. A few outrageous examples:
- Banana Cream Pie: 1,270 calories, 21g sat fat
- Reese's® Peanut Butter Cup: 1,020 calories, 22g sat fat
- Georgia Mud Fudge®: 1,180 calories, 22g sat fat

lose it!
90
CALORIES SAVED

✘ *Skip It*
Snickers® Blizzard Treat *(small)*
610 calories, 12g sat fat, 280mg sodium, 78g sugar

✔ *Choose It*
Butterfinger® Blizzard *(small)*
520 calories, 11g sat fat, 240mg sodium, 60g sugar

 ORDER SMART *Go Mini*

Downsize your Blizzard by ordering a "mini" and save a tremendous amount of calories. Most mini versions are almost half the calories of a small: The mini Oreo Cookies Blizzard Treat is 380 calories, the mini Snickers Blizzard is 370, and the mini Reese's Cup is 360.

DENNY'S®

As with most restaurants' desserts, the problem with Denny's treats is size: Most are decadently huge portions. But you can always request customizations. For example: Choose a brownie with either vanilla ice cream or hot fudge sauce (instead of both) or a smaller banana split.

lose it!
260
CALORIES SAVED

✘ *Skip It*
Caramel Apple Crisp
740 calories, 9g sat fat, 570mg sodium, 89g sugar

✔ *Choose It*
Apple Pie
480 calories, 9g sat fat, 580mg sodium, 35g sugar

 NUTRITION ALERT *A Nutritious Dessert*
Believe it or not, a dessert can add some valuable vitamins and minerals to your meal. Your best bet is a banana split with just one scoop of ice cream and a half portion of nuts (instead of the deluxe version with three scoops, three toppings, whipped cream, and nuts). The banana offers potassium, the ice cream calcium, and the nuts a bit of healthy fat.

 ORDER SMART *Build Your Own Sundae*
This dessert option is the ultimate choice since you can control portion size and toppings. Denny's breaks down the calorie count of each one so you can choose wisely. Here's an overview:
• Glazed pecans: 200 calories, 1g sat fat, 135mg sodium, 13g sugar
• Chopped nuts: 190 calories, 3g sat fat, 0mg sodium, 1g sugar
• Caramel topping: 190 calories, 0.5g sat fat, 110mg sodium, 33g sugar
• Chocolate topping: 110 calories, 0g sat fat, 110mg sodium, 21g sugar

✗ *Skip It*

Strawberry Milkshake with Whipped Cream

600 calories, 17g sat fat, 300mg sodium

✗ *Skip It*

Banana Split with 3 Scoops

810 calories, 19g sat fat, 190mg sodium, 95g sugar

✗ *Skip It*

Hot Fudge Brownie à la Mode

830 calories, 17g sat fat, 520mg sodium, 95g sugar

lose it!
269
CALORIES
SAVED

✔ *Choose It*

Vanilla Ice Cream with Strawberry Topping

(1 scoop)
331 calories, 9g sat fat, 77mg sodium

lose it!
300
CALORIES
SAVED

✔ *Choose It*

New York Style Cheesecake

510 calories, 20g sat fat, 370mg sodium, 31g sugar

lose it!
371
CALORIES
SAVED

✔ *Choose It*

Chocolate Ice Cream with Hot Fudge Topping

459 calories, 16g sat fat, 162mg sodium

MCDONALD'S®

Luckily at McDonald's "snack" means "small"—so most items on their snack menu are just-right, calorie-controlled portions. Many of their sides and smaller add-on items (like apple slices) are also great for satisfying a snack attack.

lose it!
80
CALORIES
SAVED

✗ *Skip It*
Crispy Chipotle BBQ Snack Wrap®
340 calories, 4.5g sat fat, 780mg sodium

✓ *Choose It*
Grilled Chipotle BBQ Snack Wrap
260 calories, 3.5g sat fat, 700mg sodium

ORDER SMART *Build Your Own Snack*

A surprisingly healthy and delicious McDonald's munchie: two bags of apple slices with a jug of fat-free chocolate milk. For just 150 calories, 0g sat fat, and 135mg sodium, you're getting 9g fiber and one-third of your daily calcium needs. A great choice for kids, too!

✘ *Skip It*
Crispy Honey Mustard Snack Wrap

330 calories, 4.5g sat fat, 730mg sodium

✘ *Skip It*
Baked Hot Apple Pie

250 calories, 7g sat fat, 170mg sodium, 13g sugar

lose it!
**80
CALORIES
SAVED**

✔ *Choose It*
4-piece Chicken McNuggets® with honey mustard sauce

250 calories, 3g sat fat, 475mg sodium

lose it!
**100
CALORIES
SAVED**

✔ *Choose It*
Soft Baked Oatmeal Raisin Cookie

150 calories, 2.5g sat fat, 135mg sodium, 13g sugar

MCDONALD'S®

A surprising fact about McDonald's sweet treats: They use reduced-fat vanilla ice cream in their shakes, cones, and McFlurrys, so it's really the size and mix-ins of these desserts that ramp up the calorie and fat counts. Case in point: A plain vanilla soft-serve cone is an admirable 170 calories and 3g saturated fat. Check out your other good choices.

lose it!
140
CALORIES SAVED

✗ Skip It
McFlurry® with M&M's®
650 calories, 14g sat fat, 180mg sodium, 89g sugar

✓ Choose It
McFlurry with Oreo® cookies
510 calories, 9g sat fat, 280mg sodium, 64g sugar

 NUTRITION ALERT
That Has How Many Calories?!
Thanks to their super-sized options, the shakes at McDonald's are not a great choice. The 16-ounce chocolate shake has 700 calories and 12g sat fat, while the 22-ounce has 850 calories and 15g sat fat!

 NUTRITION ALERT *Add Peanuts*
For just 40 calories, you can top off your sundae with a sprinkle of peanuts. They add crunch, good fats, and 1 gram of protein.

✘ *Skip It*

McCafé® Chocolate
Shake *(12 ounces}*

560 calories, 10g sat fat, 240mg
sodium, 77g sugar

✘ *Skip It*

McCafé Strawberry
Shake *(12 ounces}*

550 calories, 10g sat fat, 160mg
sodium, 79g sugar

✘ *Skip It*

McCafé Vanilla Shake
(12 ounces}

530 calories, 10g sat fat, 160mg
sodium, 63g sugar

lose it!
230
**CALORIES
SAVED**

✔ *Choose It*

Hot Fudge Sundae

330 calories, 7g sat fat, 170mg
sodium, 48g sugar

lose it!
270
**CALORIES
SAVED**

✔ *Choose It*

Strawberry Sundae

280 calories, 4g sat fat, 85mg
sodium, 45g sugar

lose it!
360
**CALORIES
SAVED**

✔ *Choose It*

Vanilla Cone

170 calories, 3g sat fat, 70mg
sodium, 20g sugar

OLIVE GARDEN^{SM}

*What's dinner at Olive Garden without a delicious dessert? The good news is
many traditional Italian treats don't have such a bad nutritional profile.*

lose it!
330
**CALORIES
SAVED**

✗ *Skip It*
Lemon Cream Cake
560 calories, 16g sat fat, 730mg sodium

✓ *Choose It*
Limoncello Mousse Dolcini
230 calories, 8g sat fat, 70mg sodium

NUTRITION ALERT *Portion Police*
Gigantic portions are a big reason for over-the-top
calorie counts on these after-dinner treats. Even
though the tiramisù is a better choice than the
zeppoli, it's still high in calories and sat fat. Split it
in half and share with your dinner partner or have
the server wrap up the other half immediately and
enjoy it the next night.

ORDER SMART *Dig into the Dolcini*
At Olive Garden, the *dolcini*—which means little
desserts—are usually a safe bet since they're smaller
than the rest of the dessert options. They're basically
little parfaits with layers of cake, mousse, pastry
cream, and berries that are every bit as satisfying as
some of the higher-calorie options on the menu. The
good news: All are under 300 calories.

✖ *Skip It*
Zeppoli
920 calories, 3.5g sat fat, 590mg sodium

✖ *Skip It*
Black Tie Mousse Cake
770 calories, 31g sat fat, 280mg sodium

✖ *Skip It*
White Chocolate Raspberry Cheesecake
890 calories, 36g sat fat, 490mg sodium

lose it!
450
CALORIES
SAVED

✔ *Choose It*
Tiramisù
470 calories, 17g sat fat, 120mg sodium

lose it!
500
CALORIES
SAVED

✔ *Choose It*
Dark Chocolate Caramel Cream Dolcini
270 calories, 8g sat fat, 140mg sodium

lose it!
680
CALORIES
SAVED

✔ *Choose It*
Strawberry and White Chocolate Cake Dolcini
210 calories, 6g sat fat, 70mg sodium

STARBUCKS®

A cup of coffee and a sweet treat can be a satisfying snack, but it can also be low in nutrition and high in calories and carbohydrates. Ideally, if you're going for a bread-based nibble, pair it with a small low-fat latte so you'll get some protein from the milk.

lose it!
180
CALORIES SAVED

✘ Skip It
Cranberry Orange Scone
420 calories, 9g sat fat, 430mg sodium, 26g sugar

✔ Choose It
Petit Vanilla Bean Scone *(2 scones)*
240 calories, 4g sat fat, 150mg sodium, 18g sugar

 NUTRITION ALERT
Watch Out for "Reduced-Fat"
Often lower-fat content doesn't necessarily mean less calories, and this holds true at Starbucks. Many of their reduced-fat cakes—including the reduced-fat coffee cake and reduced-fat banana chip coffee cake—are 300 calories or more with only slightly less saturated fat than other "regular" items.

NUTRITION ALERT *Multigrain Bagel*
Bagels aren't just breakfast fare—with the right spread, a bagel can make a great snack. A Starbucks multigrain bagel has 290 calories, so half a bagel with 1 tablespoon of peanut butter makes for a high-fiber, high-protein, overall nutritious snack.

✗ *Skip It*
Old-Fashioned Glazed Doughnut
480 calories, 13g sat fat, 410mg sodium, 30g sugar

✗ *Skip It*
Mallorca Sweet Bread
420 calories, 12g sat fat, 600mg sodium, 12g sugar

lose it!
60
CALORIES SAVED

✔ *Choose It*
Banana Nut Bread
420 calories, 3g sat fat, 350mg sodium, 31g sugar

lose it!
160
CALORIES SAVED

✔ *Choose It*
Croissant
260 calories, 9g sat fat, 320mg sodium, 6g sugar

STARBUCKS®

A sweet treat pairs perfectly with a cup of coffee, and Starbucks has many delicious cakes, cookies, and baked goods to choose from. Pay close attention to calorie counts: Many of the low-fat options at Starbucks aren't that much lower in calories.

 lose it!
120
CALORIES SAVED

✘ *Skip It*
Raspberry Swirl Pound Cake
420 calories, 8g sat fat, 460mg sodium, 47g sugar

✔ *Choose It*
Cheesecake Brownie
300 calories, 10g sat fat, 160mg sodium, 23g sugar

 RIGHT-SIZE-IT *Pick Petite*

Sweet treats are so, well, sweet, that eating a smaller portion doesn't mean missing out on flavor. Many items at Starbucks come in downsized versions. For example, there are several regular-sized scones, most of which clock in at over 400 calories, but there's also the petite vanilla bean scone for 120 calories. Pair it with a small coffee with skim milk, and you have a perfect treat!

ORDER SMART *Two More Good Options*

As you're browsing the sweets at Starbucks, take note of these two, which are both under 300 calories and have 3g sat fat or less:
• Marshmallow Dream Bar: 240 calories, 3g sat fat, 260mg sodium
• Flourless Chewy Chocolate Cookie: 170 calories, 2.5g sat fat, 110mg sodium

✖ *Skip It*
Iced Lemon Pound Cake
470 calories, 9g sat fat, 310mg sodium, 42g sugar

✖ *Skip It*
Chocolate Chip Cookie
320 calories, 9g sat fat, 250mg sodium, 27g sugar

lose it!
70
CALORIES
SAVED

✔ *Choose It*
Morning Bun
400 calories, 8g sat fat, 420mg sodium, 25g sugar

lose it!
100
CALORIES
SAVED

✔ *Choose It*
Oatmeal Cookie
220 calories, 5g sat fat, 150mg sodium, 16g sugar

TGI FRIDAYS℠

Fridays has all the classics—cheesecake, a brownie sundae, and chocolate peanut butter pie—plus a few signature desserts including a salted caramel cake. It's pretty easy to over-in-dulge, especially since the portions are huge. So whatever you order, share with a friend or two.

lose it!
700
CALORIES SAVED

✖ *Skip It*
Brownie Obsession®

Fridays version of a brownie sundae defines deca-dent: A huge warm brownie made with Ghirardelli chocolate-fudge sauce and topped with vanilla ice cream, caramel sauce, and pecans packs a day's worth of calories and triple the amount of saturated fat.

1,200 calories, 32g sat fat, 480mg sodium

✔ *Choose It*
Oreo® Madness

This cookies-and-cream ice cream sandwiched between an Oreo cookie crust is relatively low in calories. Split it with a friend to help bump these numbers lower while still satisfying your craving for something sweet.

500 calories, 10g sat fat, 330mg sodium

WENDY'S®

At Wendy's, dessert is all about the famous delicious Frosty. And you can get way more than the classic creamy Frosty these days. Wendy's now offers the Frosty as a shake, float, and cone. Luckily, this frozen dessert won't do major diet damage—as long as you choose wisely.

lose it!
650
CALORIES SAVED

✖ Skip It
Caramel Frosty™ Shake *(large)*

As you can probably guess, size does this dessert in, but so does the infusion of caramel sauce, which contains high-fructose corn syrup and heavy cream. The large dollop of whipped cream on top cranks up the calories and fat, adding 2.5g saturated fat. And the 153g sugar will give anyone a sugar high. Even the small clocks in at 650 calories and 9g sat fat.

990 calories, 11g sat fat, 510mg sodium, 153g sugar

✔ Choose It
Classic Chocolate Frosty *(small)*

The original Frosty really has a lot going for it. The small is a reasonable, satisfying size that gives you plenty creamy, rich deliciousness. It also offers a small bit of nutrition with 30% of your daily calcium, 8% of your iron needs, and 3g of fiber. Not too shabby for a frozen chocolate treat!

340 calories, 6g sat fat, 160mg sodium, 46g sugar

CHOOSE WISELY.
BEVERAGES CAN BE
A MAJOR SOURCE OF
ADDED SUGAR SO BE
AWARE OF WHAT YOU
ARE DRINKING.

BEVERAGES

Call them liquid energy: Drinks are crucial to our very being. Thankfully, hydration has come a long way from water, and there are plenty of delicious ways we can get the H2O we need. But beware: Some beverages can be loaded with sugar and calories and not much nutrition. Here's how to sip smart.

ICED TEA

All types of tea—black, green, white—contain antioxidants called polyphenols and flavonoids, which research shows may help reduce the risk of heart disease, heart attack, stroke, and certain types of cancer. But the key is to drink it with as little sugar as possible.

lose it!
90
CALORIES SAVED

✘ *Skip It*
Snapple® Iced Tea

Most bottled iced teas are super-sweet with lots of added sugar. And many come in 16-ounce containers that have more than one serving, so read labels carefully and be sure you know exactly how much you're actually getting.

150 calories, 0g sat fat, 10mg sodium, 36g sugar

✔ *Choose It*
Honest® Lemon Tea

This line of teas labeled "just a tad sweet" is exactly that. Honest uses organic cane juice to sweeten their teas and doesn't go overboard, which keeps their teas at 60 to 70 calories. The best part? The calorie count is for the entire bottle, so you don't have to do the nutritional math before quenching your thirst with the full 16 ounces.

60 calories, 0g sat fat, 10mg sodium, 16g sugar

lose it!
150
CALORIES
SAVED

lose it!
147
CALORIES
SAVED

✔ *Choose It*
Starbucks® Teavana® Shaken
Black Iced Tea *(unsweetened)*

It's hard to find bottled iced teas with no sugar and no artificial sweeteners, so your best bet is going to a fast-food place where you can find an unsweetened option. This black tea is shaken with ice for a refreshingly cool drink.

0 calories, 0g sat fat, 0mg sodium, 0g sugar

✔ *Choose It*
Brew Your Own

One of the healthiest ways to enjoy tea is to make it yourself so you can control the added sugar (or omit it altogether). Add a bit of citrus juice—a squeeze of orange and lemon are both tasty—for flavor with minimal calories and zero sugar.

3 calories, 0g sat fat, 7mg sodium, 0g sugar

 NUTRITION ALERT *Added Sugars*

Bottled tea and other drinks often contain added sugars, which are sugars that aren't found naturally in foods, but are added during processing. Whether they're from a natural source like honey or a processed source like corn syrup, you should limit the amount you consume because they add empty calories. Watch out for ingredients like corn sweetener, corn syrup, dextrose, fructose, fruit juice concentrate, glucose, high-fructose corn syrup, honey, invert sugar, lactose, maltose, malt syrup, molasses, raw sugar, and sucrose.

JUICE

Fruit juice can be a good way to add extra nutrients to your daily diet since it is sometimes hard to fit in as much fresh produce as experts advise. An 8-ounce glass (just 1 cup of juice) counts as one serving of a fruit or vegetable.

lose it!
190
CALORIES SAVED

✘ *Skip It*
Odwalla® Strawberry C-Monster™ Fruit Smoothie *(15.2 oz.)*

Thanks to a combination of orange juice, strawberry puree, apple juice, and grape juice, this smoothie gives you a mega-dose of vitamin C. But even though this beverage doesn't contain any fat, you do get a hefty sugar load (54g).

300 calories, 0g sat fat, 30mg sodium, 54g sugar

✔ *Choose It*
100% Orange Juice

When it comes to juice, the healthiest bet is 100% juice in an 8-ounce portion. A glass of 100% pure juice is an excellent source of vitamins and minerals; some choices are enhanced with extra vitamins (such as vitamin C), minerals (such as calcium), and omega-3s. These juices may be an even better option if they're fortified with nutrients you don't get enough of in your normal diet. Blended juice drinks can be healthy choices, too, as long as the flavors included are 100% juice.

110 calories, 0g sat fat, 0g sodium, 22g sugar

SHOP SMART FOR JUICES

• **100% PURE** The less processed, the better. Pure fruit and vegetable juices have many of the vitamins and minerals of whole fruit—just be sure to look for 100% pure on the label. Juice drinks or juice cocktails may look like the real deal, but can contain as little as 10% juice, plus they often have loads of added sugar and calories.

• **"FROM CONCENTRATE"** Juice made from concentrate is the same as the original juice. The only thing missing is most of the water. Extracting water reduces juice volume and weight, making it easier to ship. When water is added back to the concentrate, the product is labeled "reconstituted" or "made from concentrate" and generally has the same nutrition profile as the original juice. The exception: If sugar is added when the juice is reconstituted. Check the ingredients list to be sure.

• **SERVINGS** Juice is a concentrated source of calories with less fiber than a serving of fruit or vegetables, so watch your portion size to keep liquid calories to a minimum. The average bottle of juice is 16 ounces or two servings, and contains more than 200 calories, so it is easy to overdo it. Stick to a smart 8-ounce serving.

• **VEGETABLE JUICE** About 50 calories for an 8-ounce glass, vegetable juice is a lower-calorie choice than many fruit juices. But, a word of warning: Many vegetable juices can contain a good amount of salt which acts as a preservative and flavor enhancer. One 8-ounce serving can have 550-plus milligrams, and even the reduced-sodium options still contain more than 100mg per 8 ounces. Look for brands that offer the lowest amount of sodium and stick to the suggested portion sizes.

 NUTRITION ALERT *Disadvantages of Juice*

While juices provide many of the benefits you get from eating fresh fruits and vegetables, there are some advantages that are noticeably absent. One of the key losses is fiber, which is helpful in controlling cholesterol levels and increasing satiety. Also, when fruit is pressed to extract the juice, some of the antioxidants are left behind when the skins and seeds are removed.

SODA

Soda is truly a splurge, particularly since it has few—scratch that, no—redeeming nutritional qualities. One can of soda has the equivalent of 10 teaspoons of sugar. But if you absolutely crave that sugary fizz, there are healthier—and just as flavorful—ways to get it.

lose it!
226
CALORIES
SAVED

✘ Skip It
Lemon-Lime Soda

A 21-ounce lemon-lime soda—about the size of a medium at a fast-food restaurant—has 240 calories and 65g sugar and little else, making it truly empty calories. Some soda brands are lowering the calories and sugar in their sodas: For example, Sprite® has a 6-ounce version with 100 calories—but really, your calories can be better spent.

240 calories, 0g sat fat, 55mg sodium, 65g sugar

✔ Choose It
Homemade Lemon Splash

Make your own bubbly lemon-lime drink. Reduce calories by mixing mostly lemon-lime seltzer (5 ounces) with a bit of lemonade (1 ounce). To cut calories even further, use plain seltzer or sparkling water.

14 calories, 0g sat fat, 2mg sodium, 3.2g sugar

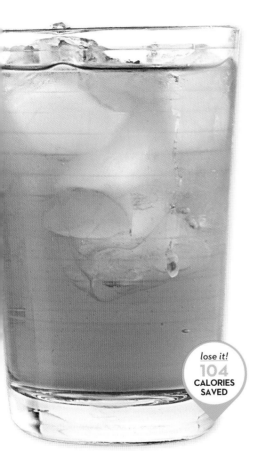

✔ *Choose It*
Real Ginger Ale

Making your own ginger ale is easier than you think.
One sip, and you'll be spoiled.

ACTIVE 8 MINUTES | TOTAL 3 HOURS, 20 MINUTES

2½ cups water
1 cup chopped peeled fresh ginger
⅓ cup chopped crystallized ginger
½ cup honey
4½ cups seltzer water, chilled
Ice

PREPARATION

Combine first 3 ingredients in a 2-quart saucepan.
Bring to a boil. Cover, reduce heat, and simmer 30
minutes. Uncover; increase heat to medium, and cook
10 minutes or until ginger is very tender. Remove pan
from heat; cover and let stand 30 minutes. Strain ginger
mixture through a sieve into a bowl. Discard solids. Stir
in honey until blended. Cover and refrigerate 2 hours
or until thoroughly chilled. Place 4 tablespoons ginger
syrup in each of 6 chilled glasses. Stir ¾ cup seltzer into
each glass. Add ice, and serve immediately. Serves 6
Per serving: 136 calories, 0g sat fat, 7mg sodium

lose it!
104
CALORIES
SAVED

 NUTRITION ALERT *Regular Soda or Diet?*

Neither. A 12-ounce can of regular soda has 140 calories,
all of which come from sugar. Diet soda has few calories,
but is full of artificial sweeteners that can increase sweet
cravings. If you absolutely can't give up soda, try sticking
with a can, the smallest serving amount available in
packaged form.

SMOOTHIES

Smoothies are the ultimate beverage in terms of versatility: They're great as a meal, snack, or even dessert. To ensure they're as healthy as possible, use fresh, whole ingredients. Making them is simple: Just place all the ingredients in a blender and process until smooth.

 NUTRITION ALERT *Freeze Fruit*

Frozen fruit creates a thick texture and a cold smoothie. Freezing your own fruit gives you a chance to use great-tasting fresh seasonal fruit all year round. The best candidates are bananas, berries, and stone fruits such as cherries, peaches, and plums. First wash the fruit and pat it dry, removing any pits and stems. Cut large fruit into pieces, arrange on a baking sheet in a single layer, and freeze. Transfer the fruit to zip-top plastic freezer bags.

✘ Skip It Chocolate Almond

½ cup chocolate milk + 1 cup frozen sliced banana + 2 tablespoons almond butter + 4 teaspoons chocolate-flavored malted milk powder + 3 ice cubes (Serves 2)

Per serving: 523 calories, 4.5g sat fat, 130mg sodium

✔ Choose It Go-Getter Green Smoothie

½ cup vanilla light soy milk + 1 (5.3-ounce) carton fat-free Greek yogurt with honey + 1 cup cubed peeled kiwifruit + 1 cup cubed honeydew melon + 1 cup fresh baby spinach + 1 cup sliced frozen banana (Serves 2)

Per serving: 224 calories, 0.2g sat fat, 91mg sodium

✔ Choose It Ginger-Berry-Oat Smoothie

¼ cup 1% low-fat milk + ¼ cup prepared oatmeal + ½ teaspoon grated peeled fresh ginger + 1 cup fresh blackberries + ½ cup sliced strawberries + 1 teaspoon honey + ½ cup ice (Serves 1)

Per serving: 178 calories, 0.6g sat fat, 32mg sodium

MILKSHAKES

Milkshakes make a luscious snack or dessert, but getting one at the diner means calorie-dense options with full-fat ice cream. Making one at home can save you money and calories, without sacrificing texture and flavor. Transform your shake into a healthier version of itself.

lose it!
497
CALORIES SAVED

✘ *Skip It*
PB Chocolate Shake

A classic chocolate–peanut butter milkshake made from full-fat ice cream, whole milk, and hearty doses of peanut butter and chocolate syrup can easily add up to some major calories for that afternoon pick-me-up.

787 calories, 16.8g sat fat, 441mg sodium

✔ *Choose It*
Espresso Shake

Combine 2 tablespoons fat-free chocolate syrup and ¼ teaspoon instant espresso granules or instant coffee granules, stirring well. Drizzle half of syrup mixture around inside rim of two glasses. Place 2 teaspoons espresso granules, 1½ cups vanilla soy ice cream, and ½ cup plain low-fat soy milk in a blender; process until smooth. Pour into prepared glasses. Serve immediately. Serves 2 (serving size: 1 cup)

290 calories, 2.3g sat fat, 243mg sodium

lose it!
634
CALORIES SAVED

✔ *Choose It*
Milk Chocolate–Almond Shake

Almond milk, fortified with vitamins and minerals, can be a delicious dairy substitute, especially when you are looking to lower fat and calories.

ACTIVE 3 MINUTES | TOTAL 3 MINUTES

½ cup unsweetened almond milk, chilled

½ cup vanilla almond milk ice cream

2 teaspoons unsweetened cocoa

⅛ teaspoon almond extract

PREPARATION

Place all ingredients in a blender; process until smooth. Pour into a glass and serve immediately. Serves 1 (serving size: ¾ cup)

Per serving: 153 calories, 0.3g sat fat, 136mg sodium

SHOP SMART *Soy and Almond Milk*

These milks are good non-dairy alternatives, but there are a few things to keep in mind. First, make sure it is fortified with calcium so you're still getting a dose. (Since calcium can settle at the bottom of a container, shake your milk well before pouring.) Second, flavored varieties like vanilla or chocolate can contain quite a bit of sugar, so read labels carefully and look for less than 14g sugar per cup.

BEER

Alcohol can be part of a healthy eating plan. Light and ultralight beers and wine spritzers don't always have to be the default choice, although they're certainly a no-brainer way to cut calories. Since quality often trumps quantity when satisfying your taste buds, it can be easier to save calories by having one reasonably sized glass of your favorite beer, savoring each sip.

lose it!
189
CALORIES SAVED

✗ *Skip It*
Craft Beer in a Stein

Sure, research shows that beer can be good for your health—but experts don't have giant beer steins in mind when they give alcohol a positive endorsement. These gargantuan glasses can hold up to 1 liter of beer. Drink too many—even light beer—and you're on the fast track to a beer belly!

359 calories

✔ *Choose It*
Craft Beer in a Glass

This is a case where a small amount of the "real thing" you're craving can end up being a good thing. One glass of a darker, full-flavored beer, even with the higher alcohol content (some specialty beers can have up to 10% alcohol, which is more than wine), can be lower in calories than two glasses of a light beer. The craft beer lasts longer since you sip it more slowly. Plus, you may be less likely to go back for a second round.

1 (12-ounce) glass: 170 calories

SHOP SMART FOR BEER

• **CHECK BEER LABELS** Guinness® Stout looks dark and heavy but has about the same number of calories as Bud Light®. Some beer labels list calories or alcohol content or, on occasion, both. It can be confusing, but know this: The Dietary Guidelines recommend the alcohol equivalent of up to one beer a day for women (two for men), defined as 12 ounces of regular beer with 5% Alcohol By Volume (ABV). As a general rule, more alcohol means more calories.

• **WHAT ABOUT LIGHT BEER?** Even thought light beers have fewer calories than regular, multiple rounds can still translate to too many calories. (Regular beer contains about 150 calories in 12 ounces, while light versions range from 55 to 125 calories.)
2 (12-ounce) glasses = 210 calories

• **BETTER BEER CHOICES** If you're looking for regular beers with full flavor and low calories, there are several good 12-ounce options:
   Guinness Draught, the classic dark beer: 126 calories
   Abita® Purple Haze, a raspberry-infused brew: 145 calories
   Hoegaarden®, the Belgian wheat beer: 147 calories
   Murphy's® Irish Stout, another inky brew: 150 calories
   Brooklyn Brewery® Brooklyn Pilsner: 155 calories
   Sierra Nevada® Pale Ale: 176 calories
   Deschutes® Black Butte Porter, a dark, creamy beer: 192 calories

NUTRITION ALERT *Dark vs. Light*
Drinking light beer is one way to cut calories, but figuring out which beers are lower in calories isn't easy since labels don't always list alcohol content and calories. Example: A bottle of Guinness Stout has 126 calories and 4.2% alcohol, while a Bud Light has 110 calories and 4.2% alcohol.

WINE AND SPIRITS

You've undoubtedly heard the research that wine and other alcoholic drinks have health benefits, but remember—drinking in moderation is the way to capitalize on the beneficial compounds these beverages contain. Women should limit alcoholic beverages to no more than one serving daily; for men, the limit is two.

✘ Skip It
Sangria
(8 ounces}
170 calories

✔ Choose It
Wine
(5 ounces)
120 calories

lose it!
50
CALORIES
SAVED

 **NUTRITION ALERT** *What Counts?*
When experts say that it's OK to have one drink a day, they're talking about 5 ounces of wine or 1½ fluid ounces (one shot glass) of liquor. Thing is, many restaurant cocktails (and when you pour at home) go over this specified amount.

 ORDER SMART *Sparkling Wine*
A glass of bubbly, whether it's Champagne, Prosecco, or cava, makes a celebratory drink that's perfect for parties. The best part: No saturated fat or sodium to worry about here, and it's slightly lower in calories than regular wine. One flute of sparkling wine is about 90 calories.

✖ Skip It

Whiskey Sour

(4 ounces)

190 calories

✖ Skip It

Bloody Mary

(12 ounces)

229 calories

✖ Skip It

Frozen Margarita

(12 ounces)

410 calories

lose it!
94
CALORIES
SAVED

✔ Choose It

Whiskey & Soda

(4 ounces)

96 calories

lose it!
102
CALORIES
SAVED

✔ Choose It

Mimosa

(8 ounces)

127 calories

lose it!
260
CALORIES
SAVED

✔ Choose It

Margarita on the Rocks

(6 ounces)

150 calories

DUNKIN' DONUTS®

As you'll see from these coffee drink swaps, at Dunkin' Donuts two things matter most: size and the type of milk. You can go with cream if you choose a small and keep it basic: a flavored iced coffee instead of a Coolatta, for example.

lose it!
190
CALORIES SAVED

✘ Skip It
Vanilla Bean Coolatta®
(small)
420 calories, 3.5g sat fat, 150mg sodium, 87mg sugar

✔ Choose It
Strawberry Coolatta
(small)
230 calories, 0g sat fat, 35mg sodium, 57mg sugar

 NUTRITION ALERT *Pick Your Shot*

Of flavor, that is. DD offers unsweetened, sugar-free flavorings which add minimal calories to your beverage (10 calories in a medium-sized drink). Choose from eight flavors including caramel and vanilla.

 ORDER SMART *The Coolatta*

The Coolatta—a Dunkin' Donuts signature drink—can pack a pretty hefty calorie, sat fat, and sugar punch; even the small runs more than 500 calories. In general, you're better off ordering a flavored iced coffee. But if you are absolutely craving the Coolatta, opt for a small with fat-free milk.

✖ *Skip It*
Frozen Mocha Coffee Coolatta
Made with cream (small)
490 calories, 15g sat fat, 85mg sodium, 62g sugar

✖ *Skip It*
Oreo® Frozen Coffee Coolatta
Made with cream (small)
490 calories, 15g sat fat, 190mg sodium, 49g sugar

✖ *Skip It*
Frozen Caramel Coffee Coolatta
Made with cream (small)
490 calories, 15g sat fat, 90mg sodium, 65g sugar

lose it!
310
CALORIES SAVED

lose it!
310
CALORIES SAVED

lose it!
320
CALORIES SAVED

✔ *Choose It*
Caramel Mocha Iced Coffee
Made with cream (small)
180 calories, 3.5g sat fat, 35mg sodium, 24g sugar

✔ *Choose It*
Hazelnut Swirl Iced Coffee
Made with cream (small)
180 calories, 3.5g sat fat, 50mg sodium, 24g sugar

✔ *Choose It*
Caramel Iced Coffee
Made with cream (small)
170 calories, 3.5g sat fat, 60mg sodium, 24g sugar

MCDONALD'S®

No need to check into a fancy coffee shop to get a great cup o' joe—McDonald's offers their menu of McCafé drinks: a lineup of coffee, hot chocolate, smoothies, and more. Here, the type of milk, the addition of whipped cream, and how the drink is prepared all make a big difference.

lose it!
150
CALORIES SAVED

✘ Skip It
McCafé® Frappe Mocha
(small)
440 calories, 11g sat fat, 125mg sodium, 57g sugar

✔ Choose It
McCafé Iced Mocha
(small)
290 calories, 6g sat fat, 125mg sodium, 34g sugar

 NUTRITION ALERT *Iced Coffee*
Sticking with a small iced coffee made with fat-free milk is the ultimate calorie, fat, and sugar savings move. Add a flavored syrup—caramel, French vanilla, or hazelnut—and the calorie count goes to 120 to 130 calories with 19 to 21g of sugar.

 ORDER SMART *Fruit Refreshment*
Check out the McCafé Cherry Berry Chiller and the Frozen Strawberry Lemonade: Both are 200 calories for a small (12 ounces) and have 0g sat fat. They do, however, have a lot of sugar, so consider it a sweet treat or snack.

✘ *Skip It*
McCafé Hot Chocolate
Made with whole milk and whipped cream (small)
360 calories, 8g sat fat, 180mg sodium, 45g sugar

✘ *Skip It*
McCafé Frappe Caramel
(small)
440 calories, 12g sat fat, 125mg sodium, 57g sugar

✘ *Skip It*
McCafé Strawberry Shake
(small)
550 calories, 10g sat fat, 160mg sodium, 79g sugar

lose it!
160
CALORIES
SAVED

✔ *Choose It*
McCafé Caramel Latte
Made with fat-free milk (small)
200 calories, 0g sat fat, 110mg sodium, 39g sugar

lose it!
170
CALORIES
SAVED

✔ *Choose It*
McCafé Iced Caramel Mocha *(small)*
270 calories, 6g sat fat, 140mg sodium, 32g sugar

Bonus: *Order this with fat-free milk and save another 50 calories and 4g sat fat.*

lose it!
340
CALORIES
SAVED

✔ *Choose It*
McCafé Strawberry Banana Smoothie
210 calories, 0g sat fat, 50mg sodium, 44g sugar

SMOOTHIE KING®

Even though smoothies are generally healthy, when you're not making them yourself you can't control the ingredients or amounts. Smoothie King has some good options, but be careful: Some are categorized as "nutritious smoothie meals" and have loads of calories—often more than should really be in a single meal. Here's what 20 ounces will cost you.

lose it!
95
CALORIES SAVED

 ✗ *Skip It*

Mangosteen Madness™ *(20 ounces)*
380 calories, 0g sat fat, 30mg sodium, 92g sugar

 ✔ *Choose It*

Mangofest™ *(20 ounces)*
285 calories, 0g sat fat, 10mg sodium, 59g sugar

ORDER SMART *Make It Skinny*

Ask for the "Make It Skinny" version, and you'll automatically knock off 100 calories. What's the secret? Skipping the turbinado sugar—the skinny versions are made without it.

ORDER SMART *Slim-N-Trim*

Check out Smoothie King's Slim-N-Trim blends, which, if you order them without turbinado, come in under 300 calories. At 153 calories, the 20-ounce vanilla is the lowest calorie choice, with chocolate coming in second at 197 calories and strawberry at 275.

✘ *Skip It*

Banana Boat®
(20 ounces)

477 calories, 6g sat fat, 319mg sodium, 77g sugar

✘ *Skip It*

The Hulk Vanilla™
(20 ounces)

801 calories, 13g sat fat, 258mg sodium, 88g sugar

✘ *Skip It*

The Hulk Chocolate™
(20 ounces)

801 calories, 12g sat fat, 263mg sodium, 90g sugar

lose it!
117
CALORIES SAVED

✔ *Choose It*

Banana Berry Treat®
(20 ounces)

360 calories, 0g sat fat, 129mg sodium, 75g sugar

lose it!
491
CALORIES SAVED

✔ *Choose It*

Island Impact®
(20 ounces)

310 calories, 0g sat fat, 142mg sodium, 65g sugar

lose it!
461
CALORIES SAVED

✔ *Choose It*

The Activator® Chocolate
(20 ounces)

340 calories, 0g sat fat, 119mg sodium, 55g sugar

SONIC®

Saving calories at Sonic is all about downsizing. Trade down to a smaller size, and you save a chunk of calories and fat. But do note that even with the smallest portions, you should still count a Sonic drink as a treat instead of a beverage to accompany a meal.

lose it!
90
CALORIES SAVED

 **✗ Skip It**
Lime CreamSlush®
(small)
420 calories, 15g sat fat, 170mg sodium, 56g sugar

 **✔ Choose It**
Sprite® Float
(small)
330 calories, 10g sat fat, 170mg sodium, 47g sugar

NUTRITION ALERT
That Has How Many Calories?!

The large-sized Java Chillers really tip the scales: the Caramel has 1,310 calories and 44g sat fat, and the medium's not much better at 900 calories and 30g sat fat. Another doozy: The gallon-sized sweet iced teas, which are all 1,000 calories or more.

ORDER SMART *Stick with the Small Slush or Low-Cal/Diet Limeade*

Overall, the small-sized slushes come in at the lowest calorie count: The Cranberry, Blue Coconut, Watermelon, and Green Apple flavors all run 180 calories, and the small-sized Grape, Cherry, and Strawberry slushes clock in at 190 calories. If you really want to keep a lid on calories, choose the low-cal/diet cherry limeade, which has 15 calories, or the low-cal diet limeade, which is calorie free.

✖ *Skip It*
Fresh Banana Shake
(small)
620 calories, 23g sat fat, 290mg sodium, 67g sugar

✖ *Skip It*
Lemon Real Fruit Slush *(Route 44®)*
590 calories, 0g sat fat, 95mg sodium, 153mg sugar

✖ *Skip It*
Java Chiller, Caramel
(medium)
900 calories, 30g sat fat, 600mg sodium, 99g sugar

lose it!
140
CALORIES SAVED

✔ *Choose It*
Pineapple Shake
(mini)
480 calories, 19g sat fat, 230mg sodium, 57g sugar

lose it!
400
CALORIES SAVED

✔ *Choose It*
Lemon Real Fruit Slush *(small)*
190 calories, 0g sat fat, 30mg sodium, 48g sugar

lose it!
320
CALORIES SAVED

✔ *Choose It*
Java Chiller, Caramel *(mini)*
580 calories, 20g sat fat, 370mg sodium, 63g sugar

STARBUCKS®

Starbucks is the place for customized coffee drinks, but this can work for or against you in big ways. The blended frappuccino concoctions can be a slippery slope. Even though plain brewed coffee has no calories, whole milk, whipped cream, and special flavorings all add up.

lose it!
220
CALORIES SAVED

✗ Skip It
Venti Caramel Frappuccino®
Made with whole milk and whipped cream

This is the granddaddy of coffee drinks. You've called in every card with the whole milk and whipped cream, which makes the calories and fat add up. This Frap is really more milkshake than coffee drink.

510 calories, 10g sat fat, 0mg sodium, 81g sugar

✔ Choose It
Tall Caramel Frappuccino
Made with 2% milk and whipped cream

Changing the size makes a major difference and allows you to keep the whipped cream. Using 2% milk instead of whole milk saves 10 calories and 1g sat fat. Switch to fat-free milk, and you skim off another 10 calories.

290 calories, 6g sat fat, 0mg sodium, 45g sugar

✖ *Skip It*
Grande Caramel Macchiato
Made with whole milk and vanilla-flavored syrup

Caramel Macchiato is a sweet treat with steamed milk, vanilla-syrup, and caramel sauce, but the 16-ounce serving packs in the calories.

270 calories, 6g sat fat, 130mg sodium, 32g sugar

✖ *Skip It*
Tall Caffè Vanilla Frappuccino
Made with whole milk and vanilla

This drink is indulgent even without the whipped cream, which, if you ask for it, adds 80 calories and 4.5g sat fat.

220 calories, 1.5g sat fat, 150mg sodium, 46g sugar

lose it!
130
CALORIES SAVED

✔ *Choose It*
Tall Nonfat Caramel Macchiato
Made with fat-free milk and vanilla-flavored syrup

Downsizing and switching whole milk for fat-free makes a big difference in calories and fat.

140 calories, 0.5 sat fat, 105mg sodium, 24g sugar

lose it!
60
CALORIES SAVED

✔ *Choose It*
Tall Iced Vanilla Latte
Made with whole milk and vanilla syrup

The latte gives you the same comforting vanilla flavor, icy chill, and caffeine boost.

160 calories, 3g sat fat, 75mg sodium, 22g sugar

STARBUCKS®

Hot chocolate is the perfect treat for a chilly day. But at Starbucks, all hot chocolate is not created equal. The key to slimming this delicious drink down is choosing the right combination of milk (whole, 2%, or fat-free) and whipped cream. Or you can always save calories by skipping the whip.

lose it!
270
CALORIES SAVED

✘ Skip It

White Hot Chocolate with whole milk and whipped cream *(grande)*

Made with white chocolate and topped with a generous helping of whipped cream, this creamy treat is the ultimate indulgence—and the calories and fat count reflect that. Going down to a tall with 2% milk (12 ounces) takes you to 370 calories and a short made with 2% milk runs 260.

520 calories, 15g sat fat, 260mg sodium, 62g sugar

✔ Choose It

Hot Chocolate with fat-free milk and whipped cream *(tall)*

It's simple but still delicious: The whipped cream adds enough sweetness so that you don't really need the whole milk. And of course going with the tall saves you major calories and fat.

250 calories, 5g sat fat, 115mg sodium, 24g sugar

ORDER RIGHT AT STARBUCKS

• **GO ESPRESSO** When you're ordering coffee drinks, the simpler you make it, the better. Your basic reasonably sized (i.e. tall) cappuccino, latte, and even the caramel macchiato made with 2% milk all have under 200 calories. Here are your lowest-calorie options:

Cappuccino: 90 calories (with fat-free milk: 60)

Caffè Latte: 150 calories (with fat-free milk: 100)

Caramel Macchiato: 180 calories (with fat-free milk: 140)

• **CHANGE UP THE MILK** At Starbucks, you can order any drink with whole milk, 2%, fat-free, or soy, and each choice makes a difference in the numbers. Going from whole milk to 2% to soy saves 10 calories for each step, and switching from whole to fat-free milk will save you 30 calories.

• **TOO GRAND?** Portions apply to beverages, too. Changing the size of your drink alters its nutritional profile dramatically. It's always best to go with the small (or "tall" in Starbucks-speak), which is 12 ounces. Or choose "short. " At 8 ounces, it's closer to a true cup and can be enough to satisfy your coffee (or caffeine) craving.

• **GET SHORT (OR MINI)** Starbucks has begun to test the Frappuccino® Mini, a 10-ounce size that is lower in price and calories than the Tall. Or order any hot drink as a "short," the secret 8-ounce size. Here's how the short hot chocolates stack up:

White Hot Chocolate: 230 calories, 8g fat, 32g sugar

Peppermint Hot Chocolate: 220 calories, 7g fat, 34g sugar

Hot Chocolate: 180 calories, 6g fat, 25g sugar

 NUTRITION ALERT *Make Your Own*

A good way to maximize the health benefits of hot chocolate is to whip up a mug at home. Minimally processed cocoa powder contains antioxidants that may help reduce high blood pressure and LDL or "bad" cholesterol. Look for cocoa that's free of added sweeteners and fillers.

NUTRITIONAL INFORMATION

How to Use It and Why

If you're trying to lose weight, the calorie and fat analysis in this book will probably help most. If you're keeping an eye on the sodium or saturated fat in your diet, those numbers are also provided. The following is a helpful guide to put the nutritional analysis numbers into perspective. Remember, one size doesn't fit all, so take your lifestyle, age, and circumstances into consideration when determining your nutrition needs. For example, pregnant or breast-feeding women need more protein, calories, and calcium. Women older than 50 need 1,200mg of calcium daily, 200mg more than the amount recommended for younger women.

In Our Nutritional Analysis, We Use These Abbreviations

sat	saturated fat	CARB	carbohydrates	g	gram
mono	monounsaturated fat	CHOL	cholesterol	mg	milligram
poly	polyunsaturated fat	CALC	calcium		

Daily Nutrition Guide

	Women ages 25 to 50	Women over 50	Men ages 24 to 50	Men over 50
Calories	2,000	2,000 or less	2,700	2,500
Protein	50g	50g or less	63g	60g
Fat	65g or less	65g or less	88g or less	83g or less
Saturated Fat	20g or less	20g or less	27g or less	25g or less
Carbohydrates	304g	304g	410g	375g
Fiber	25g to 35g	25g to 35g	25g to 35g	25g to 35g
Cholesterol	300mg or less	300mg or less	300mg or less	300mg or less
Iron	18mg	8mg	8mg	8mg
Sodium	2,300mg or less	1,500mg or less	2,300mg or less	1,500mg or less
Calcium	1,000mg	1,200mg	1,000mg	1,000mg

The nutritional values used in our calculations either come from The Food Processor, Version 10.4 (ESHA Research), or are provided by food manufacturers.

METRIC EQUIVALENTS

The information in the following charts is provided to help cooks outside the United States successfully use the recipes in this book. All equivalents are approximate.

Cooking/Oven Temperatures

	Fahrenheit	Celsius	Gas Mark
Freeze Water	32° F	0° C	
Room Temp.	68° F	20° C	
Boil Water	212° F	100° C	
Bake	325° F	160° C	3
	350° F	180° C	4
	375° F	190° C	5
	400° F	200° C	6
	425° F	220° C	7
	450° F	230° C	8
Broil			Grill

Liquid Ingredients by Volume

¼	tsp	=				1 ml
½	tsp	=				2 ml
1	tsp	=				5 ml
3	tsp	= 1 Tbsp	=	½ fl oz	=	15 ml
2 Tbsp		= ⅛ cup	= 1	fl oz	=	30 ml
4 Tbsp		= ¼ cup	= 2	fl oz	=	60 ml
5⅓ Tbsp		= ⅓ cup	= 3	fl oz	=	80 ml
8 Tbsp		= ½ cup	= 4	fl oz	=	120 ml
10⅔ Tbsp		= ⅔ cup	= 5	fl oz	=	160 ml
12 Tbsp		= ¾ cup	= 6	fl oz	=	180 ml
16 Tbsp		= 1 cup	= 8	fl oz	=	240 ml
1	pt	= 2 cups	= 16	fl oz	=	480 ml
1	qt	= 4 cups	= 32	fl oz	=	960 ml
			33	fl oz	= 1000 ml	= 1 l

Dry Ingredients by Weight
(To convert ounces to grams, multiply the number of ounces by 30.)

1 oz	=	¹⁄₁₆ lb	=	30 g
4 oz	=	¼ lb	=	120 g
8 oz	=	½ lb	=	240 g
12 oz	=	¾ lb	=	360 g
16 oz	=	1 lb	=	480 g

Length
(To convert inches to centimeters, multiply the number of inches by 2.5.)

1 in	=			2.5 cm	
6 in	=	½ ft	=	15 cm	
12 in	=	1 ft		30 cm	
36 in	=	3 ft	= 1 yd	90 cm	
40 in	=			100 cm	= 1 m

Equivalents for Different Types of Ingredients

Standard Cup	Fine Powder (ex. flour)	Grain (ex. rice)	Granular (ex. sugar)	Liquid Solids (ex. butter)	Liquid (ex. milk)
1	140 g	150 g	190 g	200 g	240 ml
¾	105 g	113 g	143 g	150 g	180 ml
⅔	93 g	100 g	125 g	133 g	160 ml
½	70 g	75 g	95 g	100 g	120 ml
⅓	47 g	50 g	63 g	67 g	80 ml
¼	35 g	38 g	48 g	50 g	60 ml
⅛	18 g	19 g	24 g	25 g	30 ml

INDEX

RESTAURANT INDEX

ISBN-13: 978-0-8487-0423-0
ISBN-10: 0-8487-0423-1
Library of Congress Control Number: 2013949510
Printed in the United States of America
First Printing 2014

Be sure to check with your health-care provider before making any changes in your diet.

Oxmoor House
Editorial Director: Leah McLaughlin
Creative Director: Felicity Keane
Art Director: Christopher Rhoads
Executive Photo Director: Iain Bagwell
Executive Food Director: Grace Parisi
Senior Editor: Betty Wong
Managing Editor: Elizabeth Tyler Austin
Assistant Managing Editor: Jeanne de Lathouder

Choose It to Lose It!
Editor: Rachel Quinlivan West, R.D.
Editorial Assistant: April Smitherman
Assistant Test Kitchen Manager: Alyson Moreland Haynes
Recipe Developers and Testers: Tamara Goldis, R.D.; Stefanie Maloney; Callie Nash; Karen Rankin
Food Stylists: Nathan Carrabba, Victoria E. Cox, Margaret Monroe Dickey, Catherine Crowell Steele
Photo Editor: Kellie Lindsey
Senior Photographer: Hélène Dujardin
Senior Photo Stylists: Kay E. Clarke, Mindi Shapiro Levine
Production Manager: Theresa Beste-Farley
Associate Production Manager: Kimberly Marshall

Contributors
Writer: Amy Brightfield
Assistant Project Editor: Melissa Brown

Designer: Ben Margherita
Compositor: Carol Damsky
Copy Editors: Jacqueline Giovanelli, Deri Reed
Proofreader: Adrienne Davis
Indexer: Mary Ann Laurens
Fellows: Laura Arnold, Ali Carruba, Kylie Dazzo, Nicole Fisher, Loren Lorenzo, Amy Pinney, Anna Ramia, Deanna Sakal, Caroline Smith, Amanda Widis, Tonya West
Food Stylist: Erica Hopper
Photographers: Johnny Autry, Jim Bathie
Photo Stylists: Charlotte Autry, Mary Clayton Carl, Lydia DeGaris Pursell, Leslie Simpson

Cooking Light®
Editor: Hunter Lewis
Creative Director: Dimity Jones
Executive Editor, Food: Ann Taylor Pittman
Executive Editor, Digital: Allison Long Lowery
Senior Food Editors: Timothy Q. Cebula, Cheryl Slocum
Senior Editor: Cindy Hatcher
Nutrition Editor: Sidney Fry, M.S., R.D.
Associate Food Editor: Hannah Klinger
Assistant Editor: Kimberly Holland
Assistant Food Editor: Darcy Lenz
Art Directors: Rachel Cardina Lasserre, Sheri Wilson
Senior Designer: Hagen Stegall Baker
Designer: Nicole Gerrity
Tablet Designer: Daniel Boone
Photo Editor: Amy Delaune
Senior Photographer: Randy Mayor
Chief Food Stylist: Kellie Gerber Kelley
Assistant Prop Stylists: Lindsey Lower, Claire Spollen
Food Styling Assistant: Blakeslee Wright Giles
Recipe Testers and Developers: Robin Bashinsky, Adam Hickman, Deb Wise
Production Director: Liz Rhoades
Production Editor: Hazel Reynolds Eddins
Production Coordinator: Christina Harrison
Copy Director: Susan Roberts McWilliams
Copy Editor: Kate Johnson
Office Manager: Alice Summerville
CookingLight.com Editor: Mallory Daugherty Brasseale
CookingLight.com Assistant Editor/Producer: Michelle Klug

Time Home Entertainment Inc.
Vice President and Associate Publisher: Margot Schupf
Vice President, Finance: Vandana Patel
Executive Director, Marketing Services: Carol Pittard
Publishing Director: Megan Pearlman
Assistant General Counsel: Simone Procas